CHALLENGES AND CHOICES

Using Creative Stories To Identify And Resolve Middle Grades Issues

Stories by Nancy Ullinskey
Activities by Nancy Ullinskey and Lorri Hibbert

Incentive Publications, Inc.
Nashville, Tennessee

Cover and Illustrations by Marta Drayton
Edited by Leslie Britt

Library of Congress Catalog Card Number: 94-77093
ISBN 0-86530-297-9

PRINTED IN THE UNITED STATES OF AMERICA

Table of Contents

INTRODUCTION

You and your students are about to enter the fictitious world of Jerome Middle School. The students who attend Jerome are very much like the students at your school and are faced with many of the same issues.

As you and your students read each story, you will become personally acquainted with Rob, Jason, Melanie, Jennie, and many other characters. Since each story features some of the same characters, even reluctant readers will find them easy to comprehend—the action begins immediately, and little time is needed to establish characterization. Each story highlights a different sensitive issue or problem faced by most adolescents. We hope that the experiences your students share with the students of Jerome Middle School will prepare them to handle similar situations in their own lives.

Each story is followed by a set of activities which were designed to stretch and challenge teenage minds. These activities provide innovative ways to get students thinking about adolescent issues—playing games, working on cooperative learning projects, role-playing, and participating in large and small group discussions are just a few of the methods used in this resource. Very little teacher preparation is required: the illustrations, stories, and worksheets are ready to be reproduced and used immediately.

Challenges and Choices can be easily adapted to fit into almost any curriculum, including the advisor/advisee program, language arts or social studies curriculum, and integrated units.

A
POCKETFUL
OF
TROUBLE

"I think we lost them," yelled Todd, his long, blond bangs blowing in the wind.

"Oh, man, my legs are killing me," complained Rob, who had been double-riding Mark on his bike the whole way.

"Did you see the kid on the racing bike? He fell coming around the corner," laughed Jason.

"Why are they chasing us?" asked Mark.

"Beats me," answered Rob. "Who are they?"

"I know 'em," said Jason. "My brother and I and two of his friends toilet-papered the kid in the tank top's house last weekend. We were almost finished when Steve, that's the kid's name, turned on his bedroom light, opened his window, and stuck his head out. I think he saw me. I didn't tell my brother because I knew he'd get mad. We were just getting him back for the job he and his buddies did on our house two weeks ago."

"Come on, let's get out of here. They're right behind us," warned Rob.

"Your house is closest, Rob," said Mark.

It seemed like the guys almost always ended up at Rob's house. It was close to school and close to Mason Park. Plus, Rob had a whole garage full of bike tools. He even had an air compressor so they could fill up their tires when they had flats.

"We can't go to my house. My parents aren't home. I just got in trouble last week when you guys came over."

Just then, Jason noticed his bike was getting harder and harder to pedal.

"Oh, great! My tire's going flat!"

"Can we just fix his flat and then leave?" asked Todd.

"Yeah, I guess so. My mom won't be home until 5:30."

As the boys pushed themselves to get to Rob's, it became almost impossible for Jason to continue riding. Every turn of the pedals demanded more strength than Jason had. But then he thought of Steve and the other guys who were chasing them. The fear of getting caught supplied him with a new jolt of energy, and he managed to keep up with the others.

They reached Rob's house and looked down the street. There was no sign of Steve and the others. If they were still following them, they hadn't made the turn onto Rob's street yet.

Rob got the key from underneath the loose brick in the flower bed. Breathing hard, he quickly opened the front door and headed down the hallway for the laundry room which led to the garage. He pulled open the door and pushed the button. Slowly, more slowly than Rob could ever remember, the garage door rose. The boys rushed inside and threw down their bikes with a sense of relief. Rob pushed the button again, locking them safely inside the confines of the garage.

"Jason, bring your bike over here," said Rob, still trying to catch his breath.

Jason rolled his bike over to Rob. By this time the tire was totally flat, but the rim wasn't damaged.

"I think it's going to need more than air," said Jason.

"He's right. He'll never make it home unless we patch it," offered Todd. Todd always sounded like he knew what he was talking about, so the guys usually listened to him. He knew how to sound really sincere, which came in handy lots of times at school when he wanted a pass to get out of class.

"No problem," said Rob. "Turn it over."

While Mark and Todd watched, Rob and Jason turned over the bike. They were about to loosen the nuts to take off the tire when they noticed something taped to the bottom of the seat.

"What's that?" asked Todd.

"It looks like . . . "

"A JOINT!" they all shouted at once.

"Shhh! QUIET! If Mrs. Green hears us, I'm dead!" exclaimed Rob.

"Pull the tape off, and let's look at it," screeched Todd.

Jason peeled off the masking tape, grabbed the small, plastic bag, and examined the contents.

"It's a joint alright," he whispered.

"How did it get there?" asked Mark.

"I don't know. I swear, I didn't know it was there," answered Jason.

"What are we going to do with it?" asked Todd.

"We have to get rid of it," said Mark.

"But we don't even know where it came from," reminded Rob. "What if we get rid of it and whoever put it there wants it back?"

"Let's hide it some place until we can figure out what to do," suggested Jason.

"That's a good idea, but where?" asked Todd.

"Not here," said Rob. "If my parents find it they will totally freak out."

As the four boys stood there, trying to figure out what to do, they heard a car pull into the driveway.

"Give me that thing!" yelled Rob in complete panic. He looked around for a place to shove the joint. The garage was a cluttered mess. He had to think fast. His eyes flitted from one object to another until he spotted his dad's golf bag. Perfect, he thought. Dad hasn't been golfing in years. He zipped open the pocket for storing tees and extra golf balls and carefully tucked the joint near the bottom of the pocket.

Rob was walking back over to Jason's bike when his mother opened the garage door.

"Hi, Mrs. Clarke," said Todd, Mark, and Jason in unison.

"Hi, Mom," said Rob, trying to read the look on his mother's face. He wondered how mad she'd be about the guys being over when she wasn't there.

"Rob, can I see you a minute?"

"Sure, Mom."

"Hey, Rob, we've got to get going. See you," called Todd and Mark. Only Jason with his flat tire remained.

"Rob, we've been through this a million times. You know you're not supposed . . . "

"Mom," interrupted Rob. "Wait a second. I can explain."

"Rob, you've always got some excuse."

"Jason got a flat tire. We only came here to fix it. We weren't planning to stay."

Mrs. Clarke looked over at Jason's bike. It clearly had a flat. She felt bad about getting mad at Rob.

"Oh," she answered. "Well, I guess it's O.K. then, but why did you close the garage door? You can see much better with it open."

"Uh, we didn't want to bother Mrs. Green. You know, sometimes we get a little loud. I mean, nobody was messing around but . . . "

"Rob, nice try, but I know you better than that. What you really mean is you didn't want Mrs. Green to know you had your friends over here again while Dad and I were at work," said Mrs. Clarke.

"Well, that too, I guess," admitted Rob.

"Go ahead and finish fixing Jason's bike. I'm going to start dinner."

"Whew, that was a close one. Nice touch! 'We didn't want to bother Mrs. Green'," imitated Jason.

"Whatever works," said Rob. "My mom would get all worried if she knew some high school guys were chasing us. She'd ask a zillion questions and maybe even call the school."

"My mom's like that too," said Jason.

"So, who do you think put the you-know-what under your seat?" whispered Rob.

"I don't know. I wonder how long it has been there?"

Then Rob walked over to his own bike and checked under the seat. There was nothing there.

"That joint was definitely meant for you, Jason," whispered Rob.

"I'm just glad we found it before somebody at school did—like a security guard or something," said Jason.

The two boys finished fixing Jason's flat. They filled his tire with air and put it back on his bike.

"Later, Rob. Thanks for fixing my bike."

"No problem."

"See you."

"Jason, call me later," yelled Rob to Jason while he was in earshot of the driveway. "But we better not talk about you-know-what over the phone in case someone is listening."

"Right."

Rob put away the bike tools and headed for the kitchen.

"Mom, what's for dinner?" yelled Rob as he opened the door to the kitchen. Mrs. Clarke did not answer. She seemed to be totally absorbed in reading the mail. Rob stepped closer to see what she was reading. It was a progress report from his school. Rob instinctively took two steps back and was heading for his bedroom when he heard the all-too-familiar words from his mother.

"Rob, don't go anywhere, young man. I want to talk to you."

"What, Mom? What's wrong?" asked Rob, as if he didn't already know.

"This is what's wrong, young man. You are failing math, language arts, and social studies!" she lectured, holding out the report for Rob to inspect.

"Oh, there must be some mistake, Mom. I mean, I might be missing a couple of assignments, but I'm sure I'm not flunking."

"Rob, do you want to go to high school with the rest of your class?"

"Mom, could we talk about this later?"

"There's really nothing to talk about. You're grounded from the phone and TV until these grades improve drastically. Do you hear me, young man?"

"Yes," answered Rob. No phone and no TV. Well, at least she didn't take away my bike, thought Rob.

Rob knew he'd get his dad's version of that lecture when he got home from work. His father did not disappoint him. To convince his parents that he would "buckle down" and get to work, he spent the rest of the evening in his room doing homework.

That night, as Rob lay in bed, he thought about the joint they had hidden in his dad's golf bag, and he thought about his bad grades. Sleep was a welcome relief from the day's events which had sneaked up on him the way a cat sneaks up on a bird.

Rob woke up the next morning with a start. His alarm clock was blaring. He picked it up and threw it across the room. The shrill noise stopped. Rob hated waking up, but he loved his alarm clock. His Uncle Jim, who also hated waking up, had given it to him for his birthday. You were supposed to throw it across the room to shut it off. It was almost worth waking up to be able to throw that obnoxious-sounding thing across his room and not get in trouble for it.

He got out of bed and walked down the hall to the bathroom. He was in luck—neither sister was in there. It was a rare and precious moment when Rob could just walk into the bathroom without having to wait. His big sister Kelly, who was a sophomore in high school, was the worst. She spent almost the whole morning in there, and then when it was finally Rob's turn, he usually had to listen to her pounding on the door and whining the whole three minutes that he was in there.

Once out of the shower, Rob looked in the mirror. No new zits and the few that he already had were starting to clear up. He remembered how Kelly had said he was lucky to have lots of freckles because the zits blended right in and you could hardly tell he had any. His mother always said she'd kill to have long, dark eyelashes and big, blue eyes like Rob's. His straight, sandy brown hair fell forward into his face unless he used plenty of styling gel. When he was in a hurry, he just brushed it to the side and slipped on his baseball cap.

When Rob was finished getting dressed, he walked into the kitchen to grab some breakfast.

"Good morning, Rob," said his mother.

"Mornin', Mom."

"Oh, Rob, a girl called last night. It may have been Jennie, but I'm not sure. Your dad took the call."

Jennie and Rob had been friends since fifth grade. When they were both in Mrs. Gregory's class, Rob got blamed for throwing a rock through the second grade classroom window. Jennie had seen the whole thing and she told the principal that Kevin Louis had done it. Kevin had never been in any kind of trouble before, but Rob, well, let's just say Rob was no stranger to the principal's office. He had been throwing rocks too, but his rock hit the flag pole, not a window. Anyway, ever since then, Jennie could do no wrong in Rob's eyes. They were not boyfriend-girlfriend, even though Jennie was gorgeous, with long, dark hair and green eyes.

"Where's Dad?" asked Rob, wondering why his dad was not at the kitchen table drinking his customary coffee and reading the newspaper.

"He's out in the garage dusting off those old golf clubs of his. His boss wants to borrow them for a nephew who's visiting . . ."

Rob didn't wait to hear the rest. He dropped his piece of toast and dashed out to the garage, but he was too late. He got to the garage just in time to see his dad load the golf clubs into his boss's van. Rob just stood there with his mouth wide open.

"What's the matter, Rob? Why are you looking like that?"

"Uh, like what, Dad?" said Rob, trying to regain his composure.

"Like you're in shock," answered his dad.

"Well, I guess I'm just surprised to see that your old clubs will be getting some use. You know, because you never really use them."

"My boss is borrowing them."

"Oh."

"Rob?"

"Yes, Dad?"

"Did you want something? You did come out here to see me, didn't you?"

"Ah, yeah, I was wondering who called me last night."

"It was Jennie McCormick. You know, Rob, you'll have to tell your friends not to call here for a while—even your girlfriends—at least not on school nights."

"Right, Dad. Well, I have to go. I'm late!"

"Have a good day, Rob. Try to turn those grades around."

Have a good day, thought Rob. How was he supposed to have a good day when the you-know-what was with his dad's boss? Rob's mind was racing all the way to school. What if his dad's boss found the joint? What if the nephew found the joint? What would his dad's boss do? Would his dad get fired? What would his dad do to him if he found out who put it there? Maybe he won't find out. Maybe no one will notice it. It was at the very bottom of that pocket. Maybe they'll think it's just a cigarette.

By the time Rob met his friends at the bike rack at school, he was a wreck. Rob's friends really looked up to him because he stayed cool no matter what. Today he seemed different. He dropped his keys twice while locking his bike. The grin he usually wore was gone.

Todd saw him first.

"Rob, what's wrong?" he asked.

"You're not going to believe this, Todd. I can't believe it. I just can't believe my luck."

"What are you talking about? What won't I believe?"

Just then the bell rang. Rob couldn't afford to be late to class. He already had two tardies. If he got a third, it would mean a detention.

"I have to go, Todd. I'll talk to you at lunch."

As Rob walked to his homeroom, he thought that his life was getting just a bit out of hand. He knew he had to get a grip on himself. He had to figure out where the joint came from, what to do about it, and how to turn his grades around without ruining his reputation.

It took a special touch to cooperate without seeming like the teacher's pet. It wasn't going to be easy, but if anyone could pull this off, Rob could. Take the tardy situation, for example. He had to be sure to time things just right. He walked in right as the bell rang. Timing is everything. Get to class too early and you're the teacher's pet. Walk through the door a few seconds too late and you end up in detention.

The bell rang just as Rob was crossing the threshold of the door.

"Yes," he said out loud.

"For someone who has two tardies already, I'd say you were playing that a little too close, Mr. Clarke. You'll wind up in detention if you're not careful," warned Mrs. Gray.

Teachers just don't get it.

Mrs. Gray was Rob's homeroom and math teacher. She had been teaching math forever, and according to her, she's seen every trick in the book. That could be why her hair color matched her name.

When lunch time rolled around, the guys grabbed whatever looked the least lethal from the snack bar, ate it, and hurried outside. It was too noisy in the cafeteria to talk. Today they each decided on pepperoni pizza, an ice-cream sandwich, and two cartons of chocolate milk—except for Todd, who was allergic to chocolate. He had doughnuts and white milk instead. Since they managed to get a good place in line, the whole thing took them only seven minutes. That left thirty minutes for them to be outside.

Usually they sat on the side of the gym building where they could see both the basketball courts and the field. There were two lunches at Jerome Middle School, so half of the school had classes while the other half ate. Rob and his friends had the first lunch hour. Sometimes the P.E. classes were out on the field, but when they were in the gym, the kids had full use of the field. There was always at least one game of football going on. The guys wouldn't be playing football today though. They had to talk.

By lunch time, Todd had told Jason and Mark that something was wrong with Rob. As they walked to their lunch spot, Todd's curiosity got the best of him.

"So, Rob, what's wrong?"

"I'm going to be grounded for life. My parents will probably make me go to one of those drug rehabilitation centers or something."

"What are you talking about? Did your parents find the joint?" whispered Jason.

Rob explained what had happened that morning.

"What are you going to do, Rob?" asked Mark.

"I don't know. I've never done drugs or anything like that so maybe my parents will believe me if I tell them how we found the joint and stuff. Then again, maybe they'll never trust me again if they think I made up the story just to keep from getting into trouble."

"If only we could figure out where the joint came from," thought Jason out loud.

"What joint?"

It was Jennie. She was probably the only girl Rob trusted enough to share his real feelings. He knew he could tell her just about anything, and she wouldn't blab to her friends or anyone else.

Rob started telling her the story, but Jason cut in when he came to the part about the joint being taped underneath his seat. Jennie didn't let him finish.

"Don't you guys ever listen to morning announcements?" she asked.

"What announcements?" they asked in unison.

"Very funny, guys. Mrs. Baker announced that some weirdo has been taping drugs to the bottom of kids' bikes trying to get them hooked or something. You're supposed to let the office know right away."

"It's a little late for that. I'm afraid our joint has gone golfing," said Rob.

"What?" asked Jennie, completely confused.

"We hid the joint in my dad's golf clubs. His boss borrowed the clubs for his nephew," explained Rob.

"I think we should tell Mrs. Baker. That way, if Rob's boss's nephew finds the joint, freaks out, and his boss calls Rob's dad, we'll be off the hook," said Mark.

"Except for one thing. My parents will want to know why we didn't tell them about the joint. They'll think we were planning to smoke it or something."

"He's right," agreed Todd. "Still, it's worth a shot. They might believe we just panicked, which is what really happened."

"Parents never believe what really happens. They always look for some ulterior motive or something. It's like they're paranoid," said Jason.

"We'd like to believe you, son, but we're just so worried," mocked Todd, imitating his mother's voice perfectly.

"I say we tell Mrs. Baker," said Rob.

"All of us?" wondered Todd.

"Well, we were all there when we found it. That makes all of us witnesses. Besides, we'll get to miss class," Rob pointed out.

With only ten minutes left of the lunch hour, Jennie left to find her best friend, Melanie. Rob, Todd, Jason, and Mark sat around and worked out the details. Rob and Jason would do most of the talking, but they knew from previous experience that each of them would have to write out a statement about what happened.

When the bell rang, they walked over to the building marked OFFICE. Mrs. Brown, the principal's secretary, greeted them.

"Who sent you this time, boys?"

"No one sent us, Mrs. Brown. We're here to see Mrs. Baker about drugs," said Rob, knowing the word drugs would bring quick action.

"You boys take a seat. I'll get Mrs. Baker for you."

"Thanks, Mrs. Brown," murmured the boys in unison.

Moments later, Mr. Hughes, a science teacher, left Mrs. Baker's office, and the boys were ushered in by Mrs. Brown. Mrs. Baker was sitting behind a huge desk—the kind of desk you'd expect to find in the principal's office.

"What can I do for you, boys?"

Rob spoke up first, and Jason helped out. They decided not to mention the part about the high school boys chasing them home from school. Things were going along great until Mrs. Baker asked them where the joint was now. She said the police would want to take it to the station to have it analyzed. She also said she was really proud of them for coming to see her with this information.

"Do your parents have it, Rob?"

"Not exactly, ma'am," answered Rob.

"Well, exactly where is it?"

Rob explained the rest to Mrs. Baker.

"So, your parents really don't know anything about this?"

"Right."

"Do any of your parents know about this?" she asked in her typical principal's voice.

"No," they answered together.

"I see. Well, Todd, Mark, and Jason, I'd like you to write out your statements about what happened, and then Mrs. Brown will write you passes back to class. Rob, I'll need you to stay."

As Rob watched his friends leave the office, Mrs. Baker's desk began to grow and Rob began shrinking, until he was this little scared kid sitting on a chair, waiting.

Then he remembered to get a grip on himself. The old Rob returned, the one who knew how to look like nothing ever bothered him.

"Rob, I'm going to have to call your dad to see if we can locate those golf clubs. Do you know if he's at his office today?"

"Yes, ma'am, he's there, as far as I know. But, I was wondering, could I call him?"

"Sure, but I'll need to listen and then I'll need to speak with your dad and you can listen."

"Thanks, Mrs. Baker." She really can be nice, thought Rob. He would never say that to any of his friends. It even felt weird to think that about a principal.

Rob's dad worked in a real estate office. When he called, the secretary said he would be gone all afternoon showing property.

"That's the first piece of luck I've had all day," thought Rob.

Mrs. Baker said she would have to call his home that evening because this wasn't something that could wait until the next day. She said she'd call around seven o'clock. Since his dad usually got home from work around six, he had plenty of time to break the news to his dad in his own way.

Mrs. Baker had Rob write out his statement, and she sent him back to class.

By the end of the day, news of the joint was all over the school, and Rob noticed that all of the students in the bike compound were checking under their bikes for drugs. The guys waited around for a few minutes, but no drugs turned up.

"I've got to get home, guys. I want to be in my bedroom doing my homework when my dad gets home," said Rob.

The guys understood.

"Call us, Rob," shouted Todd.

"I can't. I'm grounded from the phone."

"Parents!" said Mark, shaking his head.

Rob's dad was amazingly cool about the whole thing. He called his boss at home and asked him if he could swing by and pick up his clubs, explaining that he had some errands to do in that part of town. When they checked the pocket for the joint, it was still there. His boss's nephew, as it turned out, didn't really want to play golf so they hadn't even used the clubs.

Rob set the joint on the counter. Then his dad picked it up and examined it carefully.

"Rob, did you boys have a chance to really look at this?"

"No."

"I didn't think so." Then he started to laugh. "Smell it."

Rob picked it up. It smelled exactly like one of the spices he'd seen his mom use when she was making spaghetti sauce.

"It's oregano, Rob."

The phone rang at precisely seven o'clock. Rob's dad explained what they'd discovered to Mrs. Baker. She asked him if he could drop the "joint" off at the office tomorrow. She said she would have the police analyze it just to be sure it was only oregano.

While they were talking, Rob slipped away to his room and waited for the inevitable knock on the door.

"Come in, Dad."

"Well, Rob, do I need to tell you that this whole mess could have been avoided if you had showed your mother and me the joint when you first found it?"

"No, Dad. I pretty much figured that out."

"I thought so. Rob, what were you and your friends going to do with that joint?"

"I don't know. We never had a chance to even talk about it, but in a way, I'm kind of glad this happened, because when we decided to tell the principal about the joint, I thought you would believe our story because I'd never done drugs before, and I'm glad I can say that. If we had smoked that one lousy joint, I could never say that honestly again. Besides, who knows what that joint could have been laced with."

"Rob, I read in the paper the other day that all the campaigning against drugs and all the drug information is really starting to pay off. More and more people are deciding not to do drugs, but I guess it's still every parent's nightmare that kids will somehow start using drugs. After what's just happened here, I feel a lot better about you and your friends."

"Thanks, Dad."

"Now if you could just pull those grades up."

That's one thing about parents, thought Rob. They're never satisfied.

Topic One: **RULES**
Time: 20-30 minutes

Large Group Discussion

Rob broke a family rule when he let his friends come into his garage to fix Jason's flat tire. It had seemed like the right decision at the time. When they found the "joint," however, it became Rob's problem since they hid it in his garage.

Do you think Rob wishes he had obeyed his family's rule about not having friends over when his parents weren't home?

Small Group Discussion
MATERIALS NEEDED:

- "Rules" activity sheet (page 22)
- pencil
- butcher paper
- permanent marker

DIRECTIONS:

1. The students form groups of no more than four. Give each group a copy of the "Rules" activity sheet.
2. The person whose birthday is closest to the Fourth of July is the group's recorder.
3. The student whose birthday is closest to New Year's Day is the task master. It is the task master's job to remind the group to stay on task.
4. Beginning with the task master, each member is to share with the group one family rule and the reason for the rule. Go around the group as many times as possible in ten minutes.
5. The group designates one member as their spokesperson.
6. Each group then reports to the class. As the groups report, they should mention only rules not yet stated by previous groups.
7. The teacher or an appointed student records the rules and the reasons as they are given, on the board or on butcher paper for all to see.

— RULES —

FAMILY RULES   REASONS

1. _____

_____

2. _____

_____

3. _____

_____

4. _____

_____

5. _____

_____

6. _____

_____

7. _____

_____

8. _____

_____

9. _____

_____

10. _____

_____

——Topic Two: **CLASS RULES**——
Time: 25-30 minutes

Large Group Discussion

Ask the group to brainstorm a list of people or organizations that do not have rules. Are there any? Help the group discover that adults have just as many rules to follow as teens.

Next, ask the group what rules they might need to establish for this class. Remind them that this is a class where students will be sharing feelings, experiences, and opinions on a variety of subjects. Ask them to keep in mind that they will be working on a variety of projects, including some that may take them into the community.

Small Group Discussion

DIRECTIONS:

1. Students work in pairs.
2. Give each pair of students a copy of the "Class Rules" activity sheet (page 24).
3. Each pair of students spends five minutes discussing and listing rules that will help the class to run smoothly.
4. Instruct students to try to have no more than three rules in each category.

Large Group Discussion

DIRECTIONS:

1. List the rules on the chalkboard or a large piece of butcher paper as students suggest them.
2. The class then votes on the rules.
3. Ask a volunteer to make a poster of the rules and keep it in a visible place to help students keep them in mind.

CLASS RULES

RULES TO FACILITATE LARGE GROUP DISCUSSIONS:

1. _____
_____

2. _____
_____

3. _____
_____

4. _____
_____

5. _____
_____

RULES TO ASSURE THAT ALL STUDENTS WILL FEEL COMFORTABLE SHARING SENSITIVE INFORMATION:

1. _____
_____

2. _____
_____

3. _____
_____

4. _____
_____

5. _____
_____

RULES FOR ASSEMBLING AND FUNCTIONING IN SMALL GROUPS:

1. _____
_____

2. _____
_____

3. _____
_____

4. _____
_____

5. _____
_____

Topic Three: AVOIDING HARMFUL SUBSTANCES
Time: 25+ minutes

Large Group Discussion

Rob and his friends panicked when they found what they thought was an illegal drug. It took them completely by surprise. That is the way it often happens. A friend, or someone you know and trust, offers to share some kind of harmful substance with you. What would you do if this happened to you?

(Note: Adolescents are known to abuse seemingly harmless products such as Scotchgard™, correction fluid, chlorine, acid, spray paint, No-Doz™, glue, etc.)

Pair Activity

DIRECTIONS:

1. Each student works with a partner.
2. Each pair imagines a situation in which one of them has the opportunity to abuse a substance.
3. The pair should establish characters, setting, and the substance.
4. Through role play, the pair offers acceptable ways of declining or resisting the temptation.

I OWE
YOU ONE

"Can you believe my parents? They're making me carry around this stupid assignment sheet for all of my teachers to sign just because I'm failing a couple of classes," complained Rob.

"So, don't do it," advised Jason. "My mom tried using one of those sheets with me, but she finally gave up."

"What do you mean, she gave up?"

"Well, I just made it a real hassle. I always forgot, or lost the sheet, or forged signatures, stuff like that. After a while she got sick of the whole thing and told me that I'm on my own."

"So, how many failing notices did you get this time?" asked Rob.

"None."

"None?"

"Yeah, well, my mom is having such a hard time with my older brother right now that I'm trying to stay out of trouble at school."

Rob looked up at the clock. It was 8:22 a.m. School started at 8:40 a.m.

"We better get going. It's late," warned Rob.

"Hey, Rob? Did you do our math assignment?" asked Jason.

"Are you kidding? My parents are watching me like a hawk. Of course I did it."

"Can I copy it? I didn't have time to do it last night. I'll give it back to you before third hour."

Rob wanted to say no because he knew that Mrs. Gray would give them both a zero if she caught Jason with his paper, but he also knew what it was like not to have done his homework.

"O.K., Jason, but don't get caught."

"Thanks, Rob. I owe you one."

Rob and Jason got to school just as the first bell was ringing. They split up to go to their lockers. Jason was just about to slam his locker closed when Tara Johnson ran up to him and grabbed his locker door.

"Don't shut it yet. Mine's jammed, and I can't get into it. Can I keep my books in your locker until they get mine open for me?"

Jason looked down at the short, curly-haired brunette who always seemed to be smiling about something—smiling even when her locker was jammed.

"Go ahead, Tara, only hurry. If I'm late again to homeroom, I'll get lunch detention."

Tara shoved three books and her jacket into his locker, slammed the door, and ran to catch Jason.

"Thanks, Jason. Did you do our math assignment?"

"What math assignment?" joked Jason.

Tara playfully hit him on the arm and said, "Set 54."

"Well, I didn't exactly do it, but I do have it done. That is, I will before third period."

"Could you have it done before second period? I need to copy it during study hall," said Tara, with a pleading look in her big, brown eyes.

"I guess so. I'll try to copy it during homeroom."

"Thanks, Jason, I owe you one," called Tara, slipping away to the room next door to Jason's. She and Jason sneaked through the door just as the tardy bell was about to ring.

As luck would have it, Mr. Fenwick, Jason's homeroom and science teacher, was busy during homeroom setting up an experiment, so Jason had plenty of time to quickly copy the math homework. He met Tara between classes, handed her his homework, returned Rob's copy to him, and still made it to art, his favorite elective class, before the bell rang.

Meanwhile, Tara went into study hall and diligently began copying "Set 54." She was almost finished when Lindsay Rhine caught her eye from across the room. She passed a note to Tara, asking if she could use her math paper. She had not had time to finish the work the night before. Tara, not wanting to disappoint a good friend, quickly finished copying the paper, and passed it to Lindsay. Lindsay slipped a note back to Tara.

> *Dear Tara,*
> *Thanks. I owe you one.*
>
> *Lindsay*

Just as Tara was about to read the note, Mr. Cooper walked over and grabbed it.

"And what might this be, Miss Johnson?" asked Mr. Cooper, while reading the note to himself.

Tara looked up at Mr. Cooper and grinned. "Nothing, Mr. Cooper."

He did seem disappointed when he opened the note, and it didn't say much. Everyone knew teachers got their kicks out of reading about kids' private affairs.

"Get back to work, Tara, and no more note passing. That goes for you too, Miss Rhine. I'll put you both in detention if I catch you writing notes again."

Lindsay got right down to work copying "Set 54," and Tara pretended to be studying social studies, but she was really thinking about Matt Morris. She spent most of her time lately daydreaming about Matt. Who could blame her? After all, he was absolutely gorgeous—all 5'10" of him. He had great big blue eyes and blond hair. Half of the girls in the eighth grade class were after him.

Finally, the bell rang, and the class filed out.

Mrs. Gray, the math teacher, met her class at the door with a smile on her face. She always stood at the door and greeted each student as he or she walked into the classroom. Day after day, class after class, she stood there smiling as each of her students walked by.

"Wouldn't you think she'd get tired of standing around with that dumb grin?" whispered Tara to Jason.

"You should talk," teased Jason. "I've never seen you without a smile. I bet you even smile when your mom grounds you."

"Shut up, Jason. I do not," answered Tara, loving the good-natured teasing she was getting.

As the bell rang, Rob burst through the door, along with three other students. They sat down and Mrs. Gray began class.

"Take out your homework, students, and we'll check it."

Mrs. Gray walked up and down the aisles putting zeros in her grade book for the students who didn't have their homework finished.

"Doing your homework is very important," lectured Mrs. Gray. Every day she said the same thing and every day, all the students really heard was "blah, ba, blah, ba, blah, ba, blah."

"Jason, I'm glad to see you have your homework today."

"Thank you, ma'am, so is my mother," joked Jason.

"You too, Rob. It's nice to see you with your homework complete. Does anyone want to ask any questions before I grade your papers with you?"

There were none, so Mrs. Gray proceeded.

"How many of you missed three or fewer problems?"

Everybody in class raised their hands. Everyone, that is, except for the kids who didn't do their homework.

"I am very pleased with this class, and to reward you for your hard work, I'm going to give you your math test right now without making you do any further practice sheets. You seem to understand the material well enough."

"Can you believe her?" whispered Rob to Jason. "Her idea of a reward is giving us a test!"

"You've got to do something, Rob. I can't take this test. I don't have a clue what this is about. We've got to stall her. Ask her a question."

"Why don't you?"

"Because I don't even know whcrc to begin."

Rob raised his hand.

"Yes, Rob?"

"Uh, I'm not really ready for a test, Mrs. Gray. I kind of understand it, but my parents helped me with the homework, and I need a little more time to practice."

Beautiful, he's beautiful, thought Jason. He really is the master. He knows how to work a teacher like nobody else.

"How many of you feel like Rob?" asked Mrs. Gray.

Tara's hand shot up, along with Jason's, Lindsay's, and the kids who didn't do the assignment.

"I bet you students know this material better than you think. So, here's what I'll do. I'll give all of you the test, and if you do well on it, you may go to the assembly that's planned for tomorrow during this class period. For those who haven't mastered the concepts, I'll spend the entire period tomorrow explaining it."

Mrs. Gray smiled, feeling quite pleased with herself for coming up with such a clever idea. Then she collected the homework and passed out the tests.

The next day, Mrs. Gray was standing outside her door wearing her usual smile. She had the test papers in her arms. As soon as the bell rang, she returned the test papers to the students who had passed the test. Then she dismissed them to go to the assembly.

As the triumphant students eagerly left the room, they could hear Lindsay, Jason, Tara, Susan, Thomas, and Mary grumbling and complaining as they began to take a close look at "Set 54."

Topic One: CHEATING
Time: 25–30 minutes

Survey
MATERIALS NEEDED:
- one survey form (page 32) for each student

DIRECTIONS:
1. Students fill out the survey according to directions on the survey.
2. The teacher collects the surveys and tallies them later or appoints a group of students to tally the surveys.

Small Group Brainstorming Activity
DIRECTIONS:
1. Students form small groups of no more than four.
2. Each group brainstorms the topic: How could school be different if cheating did not exist? (5–7 minutes)
3. One student records results.
4. Gather the class and share results.

CHEATING SURVEY

Circle the number of any statement with which you agree or that is true about you.

1. I have copied someone's homework within the past month.

2. I have allowed someone to copy my homework.

3. I have looked at someone's paper to get an answer for a test.

4. I got caught the first time I cheated.

5. I have never cheated.

6. I cheat often, but have never been caught.

7. I have received a punishment for cheating, and I have not cheated again.

8. I would rather fail a test than cheat.

9. It's okay to cheat once in a while.

10. I cheat whenever I think I can get away with it.

11. It's okay to cheat if it helps out a friend.

12. I have resisted the temptation to cheat within the past month.

13. I have at least one friend who has never cheated.

14. I find it hard to respect my friends who cheat.

15. It's easy to cheat at school.

16. I have felt guilty about cheating.

17. I know adults who cheat.

18. I have lost a friend because I wouldn't cheat.

19. I expect teachers and school employees to be honest.

20. Cheating is wrong.

Topic Two: MOTIVATION
Time: 25–30 minutes

Game: Road To Success

Students use a game board and tokens to travel on the road to success in the classroom.

MATERIALS NEEDED:
- game board (page 34)
- game cards (pages 35–38)
- tokens (use paper clips, pennies, etc.)

DIRECTIONS:
1. Students form groups of no more than four.
2. Place the four character cards face down. Each student selects a character card: WON'T, MAKE ME, WANTS TO, TOO HARD
3. WANTS TO begins on space four.

   MAKE ME begins in the area labeled "Off Track."

   TOO HARD begins on space one.

   WON'T begins in the area labeled "Off Track."
4. Beginning with WANTS TO and moving clockwise around the table, players draw task cards from their pile. Follow the instructions given on each card.
5. The game is over when all players have completed their task cards.

Large Group Discussion:

Ask the group the following questions:
1. Did everyone complete the Road to Success? Who didn't and why not? Who was first?
2. Did you like the character you drew?
3. Do you think there are characters like these in every classroom?
4. Were you affected by the actions of other characters?

ROAD TO SUCCESS

Too Hard	Make Me	Won't	Wants To
Off Track	Off Track	Off Track	Off Track

MAKE ME

Make Me

You cheat
on a test.

BACK TWO SPACES

Make Me

Your parents pay for
your good grades.

FORWARD TWO SPACES

Make Me

Your parents are busy and
forget to check on your work.

BACK ONE SPACE

Make Me

Your dad
types your paper.

FORWARD ONE SPACE

Make Me

You study for your test
because you will be grounded
if you get a bad grade.

FORWARD TWO SPACES

Make Me

You do sloppy work
in class.

BACK ONE SPACE

Make Me

Your mom helps you
with a project.

FORWARD ONE SPACE

Make Me

You win first place
at the Science Fair.

FORWARD TWO SPACES

Make Me

You copy
a friend's homework.

BACK ONE SPACE

TOO HARD

Too Hard

You ask for help
in a rude manner.

BACK TWO SPACES

Too Hard

You politely
ask for help.

FORWARD TWO SPACES

Too Hard

You fill out a
study guide.

FORWARD ONE SPACE

Too Hard

You get confused
by directions.

BACK ONE SPACE

Too Hard

You fail
a test.

BACK TWO SPACES

Too Hard

You don't finish your work
because you run out of time.

BACK ONE SPACE

Too Hard

You give a good
group presentation.

FORWARD ONE SPACE

Too Hard

You get help
from a friend.

FORWARD ONE SPACE

Too Hard

You come in early
for extra help.

FORWARD TWO SPACES

WANTS TO

Wants To

You study
for a test.

FORWARD THREE SPACES

Wants To

You forget your
assignment at home.

BACK ONE SPACE

Wants To

You give a good
group presentation.

FORWARD ONE SPACE

Wants To

You get distracted
by noisy students.

BACK ONE SPACE

Wants To

You complete
your homework.

FORWARD TWO SPACES

Wants To

You review
class notes daily.

FORWARD THREE SPACES

Wants To

You pay attention
to instructions.

FORWARD TWO SPACES

Wants To

You copy a friend's
homework.

BACK ONE SPACE

Wants To

You get confused
by instructions.

BACK ONE SPACE

WON'T

Won't

You get caught writing notes
to friends while in class.

BACK TWO SPACES

Won't

You don't listen
to directions.

BACK ONE SPACE

Won't

You earn a good grade
for a group presentation.

FORWARD THREE SPACES

Won't

You earn a "C" on a test
because you are a lucky guesser.

FORWARD ONE SPACE

Won't

You copy a friend's paper
and are not caught.

FORWARD TWO SPACES

Won't

You fall asleep
in class.

BACK ONE SPACE

Won't

You pretend to be sick
and go to the nurse.

BACK ONE SPACE

Won't

You are tardy for class,
again!

BACK ONE SPACE

Won't

You talk to a friend and
are sent out of class.

BACK TWO SPACES

Topic Three: **CHEATERS**
Time: 20–25 minutes

Small Group Activity

DIRECTIONS:

1. Form groups of no more than four.

2. You and your friends have had the unique opportunity of founding a new city in a land far away. Your city would seem like paradise except for one thing. You have an abundance of cheaters. Realizing your problem, you approach the Great Wizard and ask him to do away with all of the cheaters. In his great wisdom, he knows that to eliminate all cheaters would nearly wipe out the population since cheaters are found everywhere. Being a kind and sympathetic wizard, he does grant you one thing. You may choose to transform three types of cheaters into people of great integrity.

3. Your group must come to a consensus about which three cheaters to transform.

   - drug testers (who abuse their position to control who is eligible to perform certain types of jobs)
   - surgeons (who cheated repeatedly while in medical school)
   - police officers (who make false arrests)
   - political figures (who accept bribes and are guilty of favoritism)
   - airplane mechanics (those who spot-check the planes)
   - teachers (who accept bribes and change students' grades)
   - lawyers (who use sly wording to cheat in legal cases and on legal documents)
   - bankers (who embezzle money)
   - sales clerks (who steal merchandise and overcharge for products)
   - children (who grow up thinking that cheating is O.K.)
   - building engineers (who build unsafe buildings to make a profit)
   - automobile mechanics (who make unnecessary repairs)

4. Report results to the class.

5. Tally class results and discuss them.

40

WAR
IN
SOCIAL STUDIES

"Give me my hat!" demanded Todd.

"Come get it, weakling," answered Mark, hopping over two desks in the back of the room.

"Throw it here," yelled Jason.

Mark shot a quick glance in Jason's direction, but thought better of it and threw it to Rob who was just walking through the door. He caught it and quickly tossed it out the door.

Just then the bell rang.

Tara and Lindsay casually walked through the door not seeming to be the least bit concerned about being late for class. Tara was wearing Todd's hat.

Todd got out of his seat to grab his hat. He nearly had it in his hand when he was struck from behind by a spit wad. It landed right on the back of his neck. It didn't really sting, but it felt gross.

"Todd, sit down! Tara, give me that hat! All of you need to get quiet! The bell has already rung!"

"Can I have my hat back, Mrs. Macanaw?"

"Yes, but not until after class."

Satisfied with that answer, Todd sat down and began to roll a spit wad. He wasn't really sure who had shot him, but he had a pretty good idea. Besides, in this class, it was dangerous to be unarmed. Most kids tried to have a supply of spit wads ready at all times. Some students came to class without notebooks and paper, but nobody came to social studies without a hollowed out pen and at least a few spit wads ready for fire.

"May I have your attention?"

Some students were talking, others were at the drinking fountain, and still others were hanging around the door to see if anyone interesting was out between the buildings on a pass.

"Sit down and be quiet!" shouted Mrs. Macanaw, beginning to get a little frustrated with her students' lack of cooperation. The class never actually got quiet, but Mrs. Macanaw went right on talking. She gave the directions,

41

passed out the assignment, and walked around the class trying to help the few students who seemed to care about their work. She also spent almost the whole class period trying to get everyone working, a seemingly impossible task. While she was talking to one group of students, the other groups took full advantage of the opportunity to do anything and everything other than school work.

Mrs. Macanaw looked up at the clock, counting the minutes until the bell rang signaling four minutes of peace and quiet before the next class began. She welcomed these few minutes to catch her breath and fortify herself against the next attack.

Mrs. Macanaw was having a terrible year. It was not as if she had not tried to get control. She put kids in lunch detention all the time. She called their parents. She sent a letter home to all of their parents about their behavior and her classroom rules. One time she even sent an entire class to lunch detention because they were so awful, but it didn't really help.

Even the goody-goodies turn into juvenile delinquents in Mrs. Macanaw's room. Take Paul Anderson. Paul is a model student. If they were going to make student robots, they'd make them all like Paul. He's polite, smart, conscientious, and quiet. He's all those things kids try to be when their grandmother is visiting. Well, anyway, Paul got his first detention ever from Mrs. Macanaw. No one was quite sure what came over him. He actually converted his pen to a pea shooter and shot a spit wad across the room. Inexperienced as he was in these matters, he accidentally hit Mrs. Macanaw right in the ear. He got lots of high fives from the students and two days of detention from Mrs. Macanaw.

The principal has tried to help Mrs. Macanaw. She pops in from time to time and restores order, but it never lasts. War breaks out again as soon as the sound of her heels, clickety-clacking on the sidewalk, can no longer be heard near that wing of the school. If Mrs. Macanaw hadn't signed a contract, she probably would have turned in her grade book and never looked back.

She must have complained in the teacher's lounge or something because one day, Mrs. Phillips, a language arts teacher, decided she had to try to do something about this sorry situation. Not that things were exactly perfect in her classes. She taught the same bunch of kids, and some days things ran pretty smoothly, but other days were a nightmare.

Mrs. Phillips spent a lot of time thinking and worrying about Mrs. Macanaw. When she wasn't thinking about nouns and verbs, she was thinking about the war in social studies. She could always tell who the kids were who had just come from social studies. It was as if the monster in each one of them had been let out of the bottle, and once out, it wanted to stay out.

Mrs. Phillips decided to talk to all of her classes about the problems in social studies.

"Before we start class today, I want to talk to you about your social studies class. You guys are giving Mrs. Macanaw a really hard time, and you've got to stop."

She could tell by the way the room got dead quiet, and by the looks on her students' faces, that she was right. Things were probably even worse in there than she'd heard.

"She can't control the class," Jason blurted out.

"She can't really teach, either. She just keeps right on talking when nobody's even listening," added Jennie. "I hate that class."

"Should she have to fight you for your attention?" demanded Mrs. Phillips.

Silence.

"You don't have to really answer, but how many of you are frustrated with how things are in there? How many of you get carried away when you go in there and do things you would never think of doing for any other teacher? How many of you think you can do something to help make things better?"

She stood there for a minute and let them think. Then she passed out a piece of paper to each student.

"I'm giving each of you a contract that I hope each of you will sign. I don't want any of you to sign it now. I want you to read it over and think about it. Don't sign it unless you really mean it," said Mrs. Phillips.

The contract read:

> I, _____ , a student in Mrs. Macanaw's social studies class, promise to obey all the rules in her class. I will be on time, stay in my seat, raise my hand for permission to speak or leave my seat, and I will be quiet when Mrs. Macanaw is speaking to the class. I will cooperate fully, no matter how much my friends tease me or try to get me to join them in classroom pranks. I will tell no one that I have signed this contract. I will simply sign it, give it to Mrs. Phillips, and keep my promise faithfully.
>
> I realize I cannot change anyone's behavior but my own. I will keep this contract for two weeks.

Then Mrs. Phillips went right on with class. She never said another word to her students about the contracts, but the students talked about it all day long.

"She can't be serious. Does she really think the kids in our class are just going to promise to be little angels?" said Todd.

"I think it's impossible," added Rob.

"Not everybody's bad in there," reminded Jennie. "Some kids will probably sign it."

"Are you going to?" asked Tara.

"I don't know," answered Jennie. "Mrs. Macanaw isn't so bad. I kind of feel sorry for her."

"Me too," said Jason.

"Yeah, right. You're one of the worst kids in there," accused Mark.

"I'm not as bad as you," said Jason.

"You're both awful," laughed Tara. "So quit arguing. Neither one of you guys could keep that contract even if you wanted to."

"I think it's pretty funny. Can you picture our whole class just sitting there doing our work?" said Rob.

"It would be a first," said Todd.

"What hour do you have social studies, Rob?"

"Sixth period. We're her worst class. We almost made her cry one day."

"I have her eighth period, and she says our class is the worst period," said Jennie. "Let's face it, she doesn't have a good class all day."

"Does Mrs. Phillips really think this will work? We're having way too much fun in there to stop just to be nice," said Mark.

"If you were truly mature, Mark, you'd be concerned with the quality of your educational experience, like me," mocked Rob.

"Right," laughed Jennie. "The only reason you even bring a book to class is because your parents are on your case."

"That's purely coincidental," said Rob.

Everybody laughed at that one, and Mrs. Phillips's plan seemed doomed to failure.

Then it happened. Mr. Allan, the social studies Teacher of the Year, and the other eighth grade social studies teacher, challenged Mrs. Macanaw's classes to a Social Studies Bowl. It was an annual tradition that was started at Jerome Middle School five years ago, and guess whose classes have won it for the past three years?

Mr. Allan wasn't even worried this year. He'd heard the horror stories of what was going on in Mrs. Macanaw's classes, and he felt confident that his kids could win, probably without any extra coaching or preparing from him. He dusted his trophy, the one he knew would continue to stay on top of *his* file cabinet, in *his* room.

Mrs. Macanaw, on the other hand, knew her kids didn't have a chance. Sure, she had a few kids who were learning something, just because they cared about school—no matter what everybody else thought. But the way the Bowl was run, a teacher couldn't select the best students and have them compete. The day of the contest, six names would be drawn at random, and those students would represent their house in the competition. Mrs. Macanaw was from House 3 and Mr. Allan was from House 4. Everybody at Jerome Middle School was assigned to a house. All of the students in a particular house had the same teachers. There usually wasn't that much competition between houses, but for some reason, this Social Studies Bowl drew a lot of attention.

The questions for the Social Studies Bowl were made up by the social studies teachers. They each had to submit fifty questions. All of the questions were thrown into a large container. The kids from Mr. Allan's classes would be well prepared to answer at least fifty percent of the questions. Since there wasn't exactly a whole lot of learning going on in Mrs. Macanaw's classes all year, well, let's just say they weren't going to be really tough competition.

"Quiet! Quiet, everyone!" shouted Mrs. Macanaw in her usual attempt to gain some sort of control over her class. When most of the class was reasonably quiet, she passed out the assignment for the day. At the top of the sheet, she had written information about the Social Studies Bowl, but she never mentioned it during class. Not one word.

The bell rang and her students eagerly left the classroom, knocking over a few chairs on the way out. The floor, as usual, was littered with spit wads and broken pieces of pencils. No one would ever have guessed the room had been vacuumed the night before.

"Hey, wait up, Jason." It was Rob.

"House 4 is going to beat us in that social studies thing," said Rob.

"So what? Who cares about a stupid contest anyway."

Just then Joe Carson and Bob Linder caught up with Rob and Jason. They knew each other when they played on the same soccer team at the YMCA nearly two years ago.

"We're going to win that Social Studies Bowl without even trying. Mr. Allan said our worst students know more than your brains know this year," said Joe, wearing a grin that made Rob want to punch him right in the mouth.

Instead he came back with, "Your class is a bunch of losers. Tell Mr. Allan to enjoy the trophy because he won't have it much longer. Mrs. Macanaw's already clearing off the top of her filing cabinet to make room for it."

"You guys are pathetic," said Bob. "Everybody knows it's a zoo in your class. I heard they were thinking of cancelling the Bowl this year because they thought it would be too humiliating for Mrs. Macanaw and you guys."

"You liar!" yelled Jason, losing his cool.

"If you don't believe me, ask Mrs. Phillips. She's the one who said you guys could handle the Bowl. She wouldn't let them cancel it, and since she's the House Leader, they went along with her," said Joe in a very convincing voice.

"How do you know about this?" asked Rob.

"I overheard them talking in Mr. Allan's room. He didn't know I was there," answered Joe. "Come on, Bob, we'll be late for math if we don't get going."

Rob and Jason walked along without saying much. Jason broke the silence.

"So, that's what all that personal contract stuff is about with Mrs. Phillips. What are we going to do?"

"We're going to beat House 4 in that contest, even if I have to study to do it," said Rob. "And if you ever repeat what I just said about studying, I'll . . ."

"Relax, Rob, I'm not going to say anything," interrupted Jason.

Rob and Jason spread the word, and Mrs. Phillips was soon overwhelmed by the number of students who turned in a contract. Mrs. Macanaw didn't know what to think. When she told the students to be quiet, you could have heard a pin drop in her room. When she started lecturing, everyone took notes. When she assigned homework, everyone did it.

"Mrs. Macanaw, we want to win that Social Studies Bowl. Will you help us review?" asked Tara.

"Is that why everyone's been so good lately?"

"Yes, ma'am," answered Tara.

"You bet I will," said Mrs. Macanaw. She had prayed for this moment. Actually, the most she'd ever hoped for was a little order in her classes. This was too good to be true.

"Will there be questions from the very beginning of the year?" asked Mark.

"Yes."

"Some of us don't exactly remember a whole lot from September," said Todd.

"Some of us don't exactly remember much from last week," teased Rob.

"Let's divide up the chapters and make study guides for everybody," suggested Paul.

"That's a great idea," replied Mrs. Macanaw. "Tomorrow when you get to class, I'll put you into groups. There will be one leader for each group who will organize the material for each chapter, but everyone in the group will have to be responsible for at least one section. So, remember to bring your books to class tomorrow. We've got only eleven more days until the Bowl. From now on, every minute counts."

Then Rob's hand went up.

"Rob?"

"Will you do us a favor and not tell any of the teachers in House 4 about this? Don't tell anyone about how we're being good until after the contest."

"My lips are sealed."

The bell rang, the students left, and Mrs. Macanaw smiled at her clean floor.

Mrs. Macanaw made up study guide sheets. She held special study sessions before school and during lunch. She made up games for them to play that helped them learn the information that she thought they might be asked at the Bowl. The students were amazed at the way she helped them get ready. They had no idea that she could actually teach anyone anything.

Meanwhile, Mrs. Macanaw was equally impressed by her students. She had no idea they could work so hard. They didn't waste a single minute. Everyone was busy. The class brains worked with the kids who usually failed social studies. It seemed like everybody got along without any arguments. They completed worksheets, outlined chapters, and quizzed each other on important dates and names. The students worked like this day after day.

The Bowl was just four days away when all of Jerome Middle School was shocked and saddened by some terrible news. While hiking in the mountains over the weekend, Mr. Allan had suffered a fatal heart attack. He was very well liked by his students, and they were understandably upset. The whole school seemed to be affected.

When Mrs. Macanaw's classes heard the news, they felt an odd sort of emptiness most of them had never known before. Mr. Allan and his students had been the enemy. They were also the reason why Mrs. Macanaw's classes had pulled together and started learning so much. Since they didn't really know Mr. Allan, they weren't really mourning him, but rather the spark that he had provided by being the competition.

No one knew how to act when they heard the news.

"Your assignment is on the board," said Mrs. Macanaw.

"Are we still going to have the Social Studies Bowl?" asked Todd.

"I'm not sure," answered Mrs. Macanaw.

"All the kids who had Mr. Allan are crying," said Melanie.

"It's really a terrible thing. Mr. Allan was a good person and a great teacher," added Mrs. Macanaw. "I wonder what he would want us to do about the Bowl?"

Everyone just sat there contemplating the answer to that one.

"Right now, I'd like you to get into your groups and begin on today's assignment."

The students spent the rest of the class period going through the motions, but nobody could concentrate on the work.

The announcement about the cancellation of the Social Studies Bowl came on Wednesday. Under the circumstances, Mrs. Baker, the principal, thought the Bowl should not be held this year. Mr. Allan's students were going through a rough time, and she didn't want them to have any added pressures.

Mrs. Macanaw had a heavy heart. She knew the real tragedy here was Mr. Allan's death, but she couldn't ignore the loss she knew her students were feeling about the Social Studies Bowl. For most classes it probably would have been no big deal, but her classes had put their hearts and souls into this Bowl.

"We could have won this year," said Mark on the way to class.

"I know," agreed Todd.

"That trophy should be on our file cabinet," said Rob, walking into Mrs. Macanaw's room. The words were barely out of his mouth when a shiny object on Mrs. Macanaw's file cabinet caught his eye. Mrs. Macanaw began class that day by reading to her students the inscription that was on the trophy. It said,

To the students in Mrs. Macanaw's classes who
don't need a Social Studies Bowl to know that
they are winners.

Topic One: "WAR IN SOCIAL STUDIES" DISCUSSION
Time: 25–35 minutes

Discussion Questions:

1. Do you think the students in Mrs. Macanaw's class dreaded going to class? Why or why not?

2. Do you think Mrs. Macanaw enjoyed coming to school every day? Why or why not?

3. What were some of the disruptive things students did in her class?

4. List things that Mrs. Macanaw did to try to control her class.

5. Did Mrs. Macanaw's attempts work? Why or why not?

6. Why did the students agree to sign the contract from Mrs. Phillips?

7. Did your initial feelings about Mrs. Macanaw's ability to teach change by the end of the story?

8. How did the students' behavior change by the end of the story?

Topic Two: TEACHER/STUDENT CHARACTERISTICS
Time: 20–25 minutes

Teacher Survey

MATERIALS NEEDED:

- list of teachers to be surveyed
- copies of teacher survey form (page 51)

DIRECTIONS:

1. Give each student a copy of the teacher survey.
2. Ask for volunteers or assign a teacher from the list to each student so that all teachers on the list are surveyed.
3. Students take the surveys to their assigned teachers one day and collect them the next day.

Student Survey

MATERIALS NEEDED:

- copies of student survey form (page 52)

DIRECTIONS:

1. Give each student a copy of the student survey.
2. Allow the students a few minutes to complete the survey.
3. Collect the survey. The information collected in this survey will be used to complete the activities on page 53.

TEACHER SURVEY

DIRECTIONS: Rank the following statements from 1 to 10 (1 being what you feel is most important—10 being what you feel is least important). Some statements will not receive a number.

The ideal student . . .

_____ has good personal hygiene.

_____ comes to class prepared with necessary materials.

_____ does not pout, whine, or snivel.

_____ completes all assignments.

_____ is very popular.

_____ listens when I talk.

_____ follows directions.

_____ smiles and waves at me outside of class.

_____ responds enthusiastically to assignments.

_____ seldom misses a day of school.

_____ dresses in name brands of clothing.

_____ is honest.

_____ is on time for class.

_____ finishes his or her work first.

STUDENT SURVEY

DIRECTIONS: Rank the following statements from 1 to 10 (1 being what you feel is most important—10 being what you feel is least important). Some statements will not receive a number.

The ideal teacher . . .

_____ lets the students work in groups.

_____ helps me when I have a question.

_____ seldom misses a day of school.

_____ smiles and waves at me outside of class.

_____ challenges me to think.

_____ gives interesting assignments.

_____ has a good sense of humor.

_____ never embarrasses a student.

_____ knows how to get students to behave in the classroom.

_____ listens to students' ideas.

_____ is organized.

_____ lectures to the class.

Topic Three: TEACHERS AND STUDENTS
Time: Two 25-minute sessions

Survival Manual for Students: Session 1

MATERIALS NEEDED:
- blank sheets of paper
- markers

DIRECTIONS:
1. The students work in pairs or individually.
2. Each pair or individual produces one page of a Survival Manual for Students. This page should describe how to get along with difficult teachers.
3. Depending on their talents, students may want to draw cartoons or provide other illustrations.
4. A minimum of ten suggestions should be given.
5. Pages are then compiled into a Survival Manual for the classroom.

Survival Manual for Teachers: Session 2

MATERIALS NEEDED:
- blank sheets of paper
- markers

DIRECTIONS:
1. The students work in pairs or individually.
2. Each pair or individual produces one page of a Survival Manual for Teachers. This page should give teachers advice on how to make their classrooms fun and interesting.
3. Depending on their talents, students may want to draw cartoons or provide other illustrations.
4. A minimum of ten suggestions should be given.
5. Pages are then compiled into a Survival Manual for Teachers to be placed in the teachers' lounge.

MARTA J. DRAYTON

54

OPERATION BLUE LIGHT SPECIAL

"Why do you think Mr. Fenwick sent for us?" asked John Malloy.

"We're probably in trouble," answered Rob.

"I haven't done anything wrong," said Terry.

"Maybe you're a witness to something that happened," suggested Rob. "Or maybe you did something wrong, and you don't remember doing it. That happens to me all the time."

"Yeah, well, it's never happened to me," said Terry.

Before they could finish their conversation, Mr. Fenwick walked up to the front of the room and asked for everyone's attention.

"I suppose you're all wondering why I've asked to meet with you."

"Whatever it is, I didn't do it," said Rob.

Mr. Fenwick laughed. "I've called you together to see if you'd like to participate in an experiment."

"What kind of experiment?" asked Chris Martin.

"I'd like to see if we could create a fashion trend at Jerome Middle School."

"How would we do that?" asked Lindsay.

"I want you all to start wearing these jeans from Discount City." Everyone groaned as he held up an assortment of jeans that he had purchased from the bargain rack. They were all the same brand, but there were slight differences in color, and, of course, he had selected a variety of sizes.

"Why us?" asked Terry.

"You are some of the most popular and accepted kids at Jerome. Look around this room. You all have something in common—name brands of clothing."

Without even looking around the room, the students knew what Mr. Fenwick was talking about. Their parents had all complained about the high cost of their clothing, but these kids wanted to wear the best.

"No offense, Mr. Fenwick, but I wouldn't be caught dead wearing anything from Discount City," said Terry.

"Mr. Fenwick, what's wrong with us wanting to look good?" asked Melanie.

"Nothing. But how did you determine what looks good? Why are you wearing the labels you're wearing?"

The room got quiet while the students considered what Mr. Fenwick said.

"I really think this experiment will be fun and very interesting. I'm not asking you to give up your favorite clothes. I'd just like each of you to find a pair of Z-BLASTS jeans that fits you. One by one, I want you to start wearing them to school."

"Do we have to tell our friends where we bought them?" asked Rob.

"Yes, you do."

Loud moans filled the room.

"Once we have students who are not part of the experimental group buying these jeans and wearing them to school, we'll know the experiment is working."

"How do we know when to wear them?" asked Chris Martin.

"We'll establish the order and frequency today before you leave, if you all decide to participate in the experiment," said Mr. Fenwick. "Of course it's extremely important for you not to breathe a word of this to anyone, especially your closest friends. I have a letter for your parents to sign which explains what we're doing and asks for their permission to have you participate."

"What if we start out in the experiment, but our friends make fun of us and we want to drop out?" asked Lindsay.

"I've selected all of you very carefully. You're all kids who are very accepted at Jerome. Your peers look up to you. Once the experiment gets started, I need all of you to stick it out no matter what."

"How long will we be doing this?" asked John Malloy.

"Well, I'm not really sure. I think it will take us at least a month, but it may take a little longer."

More groans.

"But you don't have to wear only the Discount City jeans. I just want you to include them in your wardrobes and wear them to school at least once a week."

"We'll need to wear them places on weekends with our friends if we want them to really fall for this," suggested Rob.

"He's right," agreed Terry Baxter.

"Good point," said Mr. Fenwick.

"Does Discount City have a lot more pairs in stock?" asked Jennie.

"Yes, as part of my research I went to several stores and checked with the managers. Discount City got a great deal on these jeans, and they bought thousands of pairs of them."

"How much do they cost?"

"They retail for $10.99. I bought so many pairs that Discount City gave me a discount. I actually paid only $8.99 a pair for the jeans you'll be wearing."

"Do they sell them in both the men's and women's departments?" asked Sara Lane.

"Good question. Yes, they do."

"Did you pay for all of these jeans with your own money?" asked Melanie.

"Several months ago I wrote a grant proposal. This project is being funded by the research department of the fashion industry. They paid for the jeans."

"What if we don't want to be in the experiment?" asked Ryan Taylor.

"Naturally I'm hoping you'll all decide to do this. I think we have a chance here to have some fun and learn something at the same time, but if you can't make the commitment, then I'll ask that you promise not to interfere with the experiment and that you tell absolutely no one about it."

"Let's vote, Mr. Fenwick. I'll do it if everyone will, but I don't want to make a complete fool of myself all by myself. I want company," said Rob.

"Before we vote, there are two more things I have to tell you. I'd like you to keep a journal during the experiment and write down anything kids say to you when you're wearing the jeans, and write down your feelings too. We'll also need to meet once a week and share our experiences with one another. We'll meet during Prime Time."

"Somebody might get suspicious if the same kids wearing the Discount City jeans are meeting in your room once a week," said Terry.

"You may be right, Terry. I just thought you would need to give each other some support if some of the kids give you a bad time or something," said Mr. Fenwick.

"We can handle it. We'll call each other if we have trouble," said Melanie.

"Are we ready to vote?" asked Mr. Fenwick.

"Let's do it," said Matt.

"We'll vote by secret ballot. You must sign your name so I'll know who's participating and who's not."

Mr. Fenwick passed out little slips of blue paper. There were two choices on the ballot. The students were instructed to place a check mark in the square of their choice. Then Mr. Fenwick collected the ballots and tallied the votes.

"Two of you have decided not to be a part of the experiment. The rest of you are about to become trend-setters!"

"Who voted against it, Mr. Fenwick?" asked John.

"I did," said Darlene Karrol. "I just can't see myself in those jeans. Any time I leave the house looking bad, I have a bad day. I just don't think I could do it."

"Thanks for your honesty," said Mr. Fenwick. "Can we count on your silence?"

"Yes."

"I'm the other one," admitted Steve Lewis reluctantly. "I'll buy a pair if they start to catch on, but right now I can't picture myself in a Discount City special."

The other students laughed.

"Mr. Fenwick, tell us these jeans weren't a blue light special. Leave us with a little dignity," joked Rob.

"Well . . . ."

"No, you've got to be kidding," said Melanie.

"Sorry, guys, but that's how I noticed them."

"Hey, let's call our experiment Operation Blue Light Special," suggested Terry.

"All those in favor say, 'Aye'."

A loud chorus of "ayes" filled the room.

"Operation Blue Light Special it is," said Mr. Fenwick, pleased with their enthusiasm. He knew the experiment would never work unless the students bought into it completely. "Now for the hard part. Who's willing to go first?"

Not a single hand was raised.

"Mr. Fenwick, why don't you put our blue slips of paper that we used for voting in a hat and draw names," suggested Sara.

"I was hoping to get a volunteer to at least get us started, but if we don't have one we'll have to do as you've suggested," replied Mr. Fenwick.

"I guess I'll go first," said Rob. "I'm all out of clean clothes, and I'll do anything to put off doing my laundry."

Everyone laughed. Mr. Fenwick searched through the votes and removed Rob's name. Then he began drawing names and assigning dates to the students.

"Remember, once you've made your debut in a pair of these lovelies, you should wear them at least one day a week," instructed Mr. Fenwick.

"Mr. Fenwick, I never repeat my clothes that often," said Terry.

"See, I'm not the only one who hates to do laundry," said Rob.

"Well, Terry and Rob, we'll just have to ask you to make this sacrifice for the good of Operation Blue Light Special," said Mr. Fenwick.

"O.K., but I think it's kind of tacky," said Terry.

"The whole thing is tacky," laughed Matt.

That got the whole group laughing.

"It's time for you to select your jeans. I'll spread them out on the back tables, girls on one table, boys on the other."

"I want a blue-striped pair. I think I can wear them with my navy blue T-shirt," said Melanie.

"They are stunning," joked Sara. "Personally, I like the checkered ones."

"These are stylish," said Rob, holding up a black pair. "Black goes with everything."

"You mean with whatever's clean?" teased Terry.

"You're catchin' on, Terry," answered Rob.

The students searched through the piles of jeans until each one of them found a pair he or she could live with. None of them really liked their jeans, but they did actually begin to talk about wearing them. They slipped them into some brown bags Mr. Fenwick had brought with him, and stuffed them into their backpacks and book bags.

"I bought some extra pairs," said Mr. Fenwick, so if you get home and those don't fit, see me privately tomorrow and we'll make a trade. We're almost out of time. Good luck and thanks a lot for taking on this challenge," said Mr. Fenwick.

Rob looked in the mirror at his baggy, black jeans. "Why did they print this label so big?" said Rob, thinking out loud. "Manufacturers who make cheap clothes should have enough sense to hide their labels."

There was just no way to cover that obnoxious Z-BLASTS label. Finally, satisfied that he looked as good as possible, he walked into the kitchen. His parents tried to reassure him before he left for school.

"You look fine, Rob," said Mrs. Clarke.

"I have a really expensive pair of slacks that look just like those," added Mr. Clarke.

Great, I have jeans like my forty-year-old father, thought Rob. But he didn't say that out loud. Instead he thanked his dad and went out the door.

He rode over to Jason's house. Jason didn't even seem to notice, but then again, he hadn't gotten off of his bike yet. When they got to school and were locking their bikes, Jason looked over at him and said, "Did you get dressed in the dark?"

"What do you mean?"

"Look at your jeans. Those aren't yours."

"Yes, they are. They're new."

"Oh. What kind are they?"

"Z-BLASTS."

"I've never heard of them. Where'd you buy them?" asked Jason.

"My mom bought them somewhere," answered Rob, chickening out.

"Did she make you wear them?"

"No."

"Then you like them?"

"Yeah."

"Oh."

"Don't you?"

"Yeah, I do. Find out where your mom bought them. Maybe my mom will get me a pair, unless they're too expensive. My mom's broke."

"I think she got them on sale. You know my mom."

Then Rob thought to himself, "I've almost got a taker. Of course it'll be all over when he finds out they're from Discount City."

Rob had his second jeans encounter just before second hour. He was on his way to class when he ran into Jennie and Melanie in the hall. Melanie said hello to him as usual, but Jennie stood there giggling.

"Rob, where did you get those jeans?" she asked between giggles.

"What's wrong with them?" asked Rob.

"I don't know. They're kind of funny looking. They're so baggy. They make your legs look like skinny little sticks," she answered, still unable to control her giggles.

"I like 'em," said Melanie. "Are they Z-BLASTS?"

"Yeah, they are."

"Z-BLASTS?" repeated Jennie. "I've never heard of them."

"Now you have," said Rob, and he walked off to class.

"This could be a very long day," thought Rob. "Thank God for Melanie."

More than 300 eighth graders roam the halls of Jerome Middle School. By the end of the first week, fifteen of the most popular students had been seen and noticed wearing their Z-BLASTS. Each one of them had many interesting experiences to record in their journals during that very first week of the experiment. Some were funny; others were embarrassing.

Sara Lane was scheduled to wear her Z-BLASTS on Friday. She had been dreading it all week. Sara was very petite so she definitely had to wear the smallest size of Z-BLASTS that Mr. Fenwick had purchased. The only ones that fit her were bright green with a bold, navy blue stripe. These jeans, which were unlike anything she would have chosen to wear, overpowered her small frame. It took every ounce of courage she had to walk out the door and go to school. When she got there, she wished she'd stayed home.

Standing right next to her locker was perhaps the most uncool, out-of-style girl at Jerome, and at this very moment Sara looked like her identical twin. Both girls were wearing the very same Z-BLASTS jeans with white shirts.

"I like your jeans," said Christine Belemy. She was all smiles as she said it.

"I like yours too," said Sara, nearly choking on the words.

"Did you get yours at Discount City?" asked Christine in a voice loud enough for half the world to hear.

Sara looked around. Was it just her imagination or was everybody at her end of the hallway listening to their conversation?

"Yes, I did," answered Sara as quietly as possible.

"Me too," came the booming reply from Christine.

"I've got to get away from her," thought Sara. She quickened her pace so that Christine had to practically run to keep up with her. Christine did not get the hint, and Sara arrived at her first hour class with Christine right by her side. Thankfully, Christine was not in her class, so she had to turn and leave. Sara sat down and breathed a sigh of relief. She wished she could become invisible.

"You always find the cutest clothes," said Mary Ellen Delancy, one of the snobbiest girls in school.

"Thanks," said Sara.

"I love your outfit. Where did you buy it?" pressed Mary Ellen.

"Discount City," answered Sara.

Mary Ellen started to laugh. "Sara, you crack me up. Discount City. Right. I'm sure."

"I'm not kidding, Mary Ellen. They were a blue light special."

"You won't give it up, will you?" asked Mary Ellen between laughs. "I never knew you had such a great sense of humor. Or is it that you just don't want to tell me where you bought them?"

"I'd like to begin class now," said Mrs. Macanaw. "So I'm afraid you'll have to finish your conversations later."

"Thank you, thank you," said Sara under her breath.

By the end of the second week, all twenty of the students involved in the experiment had talked at least one person into buying a pair of Z-BLASTS. Parents were certainly willing; after all, they were cheap enough. Having their kids want clothing from Discount City was confusing to the parents, which made it all the more enjoyable for the kids.

During the middle of the third week of the experiment, the students decided to work on some strategy to speed things up. They passed the word around school that Friday would be Z-BLASTS Day. Instead of dreading their day to wear their jeans, the kids in the experiment were beginning to

61

enjoy the idea of getting as many kids in the eighth grade class as they could to wear Z-BLASTS. There were some kids in every class wearing jeans they wouldn't have been caught dead in three weeks ago, and the kids in the experiment knew it was all because of them.

On Friday, Mr. Fenwick counted seventy-three pairs of Z-BLASTS on campus. He was pleased, and so was Discount City. The following Monday he called the experimental group together for a brief meeting.

"Where are your Z-BLASTS, Mr. Fenwick?" asked Melanie.

"Well, I don't usually wear jeans to school," he answered.

"Do you own a pair of Z-BLASTS?" asked Rob, who was not about to let his teacher off the hook that easily.

"I don't have a pair yet, but after seeing you kids in them every day, I'm actually beginning to like them."

"Me too," said Sara. "When I first saw them, I thought they were ugly, but now I like them. Why is that?"

"THAT is what this whole experiment is about," answered Mr. Fenwick. "Why do you think your opinion of Z-BLASTS has changed?"

"Well, for one thing, I've gotten lots of compliments on them," said Sara.

"I noticed that when Jennie started to laugh at me when I was wearing them for the first time, she quit when Melanie said she thought they were cool and acted like they were a brand name of jeans," said Rob.

"How many of you had similar experiences?" asked Mr. Fenwick.

More than half of the group raised their hands.

"How many of you have changed your opinions of Z-BLASTS because more and more students are wearing them?"

Almost everyone raised their hands.

"How many of you sense the power you have to create change among your peers?"

Everyone's hands shot up.

"My mother always said she thought I wanted certain brand names of clothing just because my friends were wearing them, and I argued with her. Until now, I really believed that my friends and I just happened to like the same styles and brands of clothing," said Terry.

"I'm confused about one thing. Christine Belemy was wearing Z-BLASTS before we ever started the experiment. She quit wearing them when it became 'cool' to wear them. This was her chance to be cool for once, but she wanted no part of it," said Sara.

"What do you think about that?" asked Mr. Fenwick.

"Maybe some people don't want to be like everybody else," said Lindsay.

"I don't want to be like everybody else," said Rob. "But I'm no fashion expert, and I know if I stick with brand names I'll be safe. No one will make fun of me."

"Rob, everyone makes fun of you—but it's not your clothes," teased

Melanie.

"For once I tried to be serious and reveal my true, innermost feelings and look what happens," said Rob in a voice guaranteed to elicit sympathy from the whole class.

"Rob, you know I was only kidding," said Melanie.

"Sure, you say that now after my self-esteem has been destroyed."

"How do the brand names get to be brand names?" asked Mr. Fenwick, bringing the class back to the topic of discussion.

"I guess with people like us. Enough people decide that something is cool, and then everybody else follows along," said Melanie.

"Not everybody. Some people can't afford the brand names of clothing," said Terry.

"Why do the brand names of clothing always cost so much more?"

"It has to do with supply and demand. When everyone wants a particular product, the price usually goes up because the manufacturers know they can command that kind of price."

"Do you think Z-BLASTS will get to be more expensive as we continue the experiment?" asked John.

"I don't know how much of an impact three hundred eighth graders will make, but if what you kids have started really does catch on, who knows what could happen," said Mr. Fenwick.

The bell rang, and the world's newest group of trend-setters walked to their next class.

Topic One: CONSUMER AWARENESS SURVEY
Time: 5–10 minutes

DIRECTIONS:

1. Students form small groups of no more than four to share survey results.
2. One person from each group will summarize results.

Think about the last time you went shopping for clothes.

1. What did you buy?_____

2. From what store did you purchase this item? _____

3. How many stores did you check before making this purchase? _____

4. Was this item on sale? _____

5. Did you go specifically to buy this item or did you just discover it?

   _____

   _____

6. Whose money did you spend? _____

7. What factors did you consider before making this purchase?
   _____ brand name
   _____ price
   _____ quality
   _____ usability (How often can you wear it?)
   _____ cost to clean (Can it be laundered or must it be dry cleaned?)
   _____ durability (How long will it last?)

8. Whom did you consult before making this purchase?_____

9. Are you happy with your purchase? Why or why not? _____

   _____

10. How were you treated by the salesperson when you bought this item?

    _____

    _____

11. Do the salespeople influence where you shop or what you buy? Explain.

    _____

    _____

Topic Two: THE RIGHT PRICE GAME

Time: Three 25-minute sessions

MATERIALS NEEDED:

- one envelope per group
- paper
- pencils
- merchandise category slips—one per group and one to cut up (page 67)

Overview

Students will develop and play a game similar to "The Price Is Right."

Session 1

DIRECTIONS:

1. Students form small groups of no more than four.
2. Each group is given a merchandise category.

   (Note: Each group of four students will need a category. You may not need to use all of the merchandise categories.)

3. The group must decide the details of its category. Each student is responsible for contacting a store and pricing at least one item.

Session 2

DIRECTIONS:

1. Students reassemble into their small groups.
2. Students compute the total cost of all items in their category.
3. The total amount and a listing of the items are to be written on the outside of an envelope. The price and description of each individual item is to be placed inside the envelope for safekeeping until each group is ready to present.

THE RIGHT PRICE GAME

Session 3

DIRECTIONS:

1. Students reassemble into their small groups.

2. Give each group a copy of the merchandise category slips (page 67).

3. Each group selects one representative for each merchandise category. Everyone should have at least one turn.

4. The group presenting its category will not bid on that category.

5. The total price of the merchandise category is posted on the board.

6. A representative from each group moves to the front of the room.

7. Next, each member of the presenting group reads the description of the item he or she has priced.

   (Note: Information should include the brand name and the store where the item was priced. For example: "This long-sleeve Guess?™ sweatshirt features an embroidered front. It was priced in the women's department at Broadway.)

8. Players from each of the groups write down an exact price for each item as it is described. The player who comes closest to the exact price without going over wins a point for his or her group.

9. Play proceeds until all categories have been presented. The group with the most points wins.

OPERATION BLUE LIGHT SPECIAL
Merchandise Category Slips

- -

A DAY'S ENTERTAINMENT
(horseback riding, bowling, movies, etc.)

- -

DINNER AT HOME FOR FOUR
(a well-balanced meal)

- -

BOY'S CLOTHES FOR A DANCE
(brand names only, include shoes)

- -

BOY'S CLOTHES FOR A DANCE
(no brand names, include shoes)

- -

GIRL'S OUTFIT FOR A DANCE
(brand names only, include shoes)

- -

GIRL'S OUTFIT FOR A DANCE
(no brand names, include shoes)

- -

HOME ENTERTAINMENT
(TV, VCR, CD player, etc.)

- -

BEDROOM FURNITURE
(bed, lamp, bedding, dresser, etc.)

- -

68

SWEET
VIOLETS

The people who lived across the street from Jerome Middle School never had to leave home for entertainment. They merely opened their blinds or sat on their front porches and waited. Those who had lived there for a number of years, the tenacious ones, had seen it all. They had watched football, baseball, frisbee throwing, kite flying, and paper airplane flying contests. Most of them had at one time or another seen fire drills, kids sneaking cigarettes, boys having knock-down-drag-out fights, and young lovers locked in passionate embraces between classes.

One day Sara Larkin and Ryan Deaver accidentally locked their braces while giving each other a quick kiss between classes. It ended up being the longest kiss in history. They actually had to creep along together to the nurse's office so Mrs. Nelson could pry them apart without ruining their orthodontics. The whole school enjoyed that kiss. That is—everyone except Sara and Ryan. Surely at least one of the neighbors found that little incident amusing.

Unfortunately, living right across the street from Jerome Middle School also had its downside. The standard sidewalks, which most people found more than adequate, were not able to contain the groups of students on their way to and from school and other social and athletic events. Lawns were trampled, flowers often were crushed by size twelve sneakers, and yards were littered regularly with candy and gum wrappers, school papers, and important notices which parents never see.

Some of the neighbors had become rather cross over the years. Their blood pressure rose at the mere sight of a teenager. Others had kept their perspective about the whole thing, though admittedly they were in the minority.

Mr. Amopolous belonged to this minority. He had lived in the same beige stucco home for twenty-five years. He and his wife raised three boys there. Two years ago Mrs. Amopolous had to be put in a nursing home because her Alzheimer's disease made it impossible for him to take care of her at home. He remained devoted to her, visiting her daily.

When Mr. Amopolous was not visiting his wife, he was usually working in his garden. For years, he and Mrs. Amopolous had spent every morning tending their fruit trees, flowers, and vegetable garden. They were known for their prize-winning tomatoes, which they could grow like no one else. Now, Mr. Amopolous carried on alone without her, and he tried very hard not to be too sad.

Rob and Jason walked past his yard every morning, as did hundreds of other seventh and eighth graders. They never noticed any of the other neighbors, but they always spoke to Mr. Amopolous. They met one day when Mr. Amopolous was struggling with a twenty-five pound sack of peat moss. No one could ever accuse Rob and Jason of being overly helpful, but when they saw the old man straining himself, they put down their bikes and offered to help. That was the beginning of their friendship with the old man. After that, he often sent them home with sacks of home-grown vegetables, and they occasionally helped him with his yard work. They looked for him whenever they passed his house, and he kept an eye out for them.

One thing the boys had noticed was that Mr. Amopolous spent a lot of time caring for a small bed of violets. He constantly watered and fertilized them, and they were exceptionally pretty. So pretty, in fact, that Rob and Jason, who cared nothing at all about flowers, noticed them.

Mr. Amopolous always had dinner with his wife at the nursing home. Some days she recognized him and other days she didn't. It was the part about her disease that Mr. Amopolous found hardest to accept. Violets had always been her favorite flower, and Mr. Amopolous grew them and presented her with a magnificent bouquet of them twice each year, for her birthday and for their wedding anniversary. Her eyesight was failing so she could not really see them very well, but she so enjoyed their fragrance that they usually brought tears to her eyes.

One night, Mr. Amopolous nearly joined the majority. He had gone to the nursing home to have dinner with his wife. He returned a little later than usual because they were having a very nice visit. Mrs. Amopolous seemed very coherent and times like these were rather infrequent and very precious to both of them.

He said good-bye to his dear wife and drove home. When he made the turn onto his driveway, his headlights shone upon his garden, revealing a tragic sight. His violets and some of his vegetables were almost completely destroyed. Upon close inspection he could see where several large footprints had gouged the soil and trampled the once beautiful flowers.

"Who could have done this!" he shouted. But he knew the answer to his question even before he asked it. Judging from the appearance of the litter-ridden street, there had been some kind of athletic event at the school that night. He had often observed the carefree way the young teenagers poured out of the school buildings, heading for their homes. He liked to watch them because they were so full of life. Even now in his anger and hurt, he reminded himself that surely this was an accident. Two or three kids had probably gotten carried away in a game of chase.

Sadly, he walked back to his car, opened the garage door, put away his car, and went to bed.

Rob and Jason made the same unhappy discovery the next morning on their way to school.

"Jason, look," said Rob, stopping his bike.

"I wonder if Mr. Amopolous has seen it yet? He's usually outside by now."

The boys waited for a minute, and when Mr. Amopolous didn't appear in his yard, the boys decided to ring his bell. They waited for what seemed like a long time, but still no one answered. Then, just as they were getting ready to leave, he answered the door.

"Hello, boys," he said.

"Hi, Mr. Amopolous. What happened to your yard?"

"I don't know. When I came back from the nursing home last night, I found it like that."

"I'd like to know who did this," said Jason.

"We'll find out for you!" added Rob. "Somebody at school must have seen what happened."

"Thank you, boys, but what good will that do? The damage has already been done. I won't have time to grow Mrs. Amopolous some new violets in time for her birthday."

"When is her birthday?" asked Jason.

"It's next Wednesday, but don't worry about it. She may not even recognize me or know it's her birthday," said Mr. Amopolous. He was trying his hardest not to sound depressed or upset in front of the boys, but he wasn't very convincing. His eyes usually had a certain sparkle to them, but today they just looked old.

Rob looked at his watch. The tardy bell was due to ring in three minutes.

"We have to go, Jason. We're going to be late," warned Rob.

"O.K. Bye, Mr. Amopolous. We're sorry this happened," said Jason, speaking for both of them.

"Good-bye, boys."

Rob and Jason couldn't get Mr. Amopolous off of their minds. He was such a nice man. He didn't deserve anything like this.

"Jason, we've got to do something about Mr. Amopolous's yard."

"I was thinking the same thing."

"Maybe we could buy him some new violets and plant them for him," suggested Rob.

"I don't know how to plant flowers. And besides, I'm also broke. Aren't violets expensive?"

"Probably," said Rob.

"Let's bring it up for discussion during Prime Time today. Mrs. Gray said we should feel free to bring up any problems we have to the group for help," suggested Jason.

"Excellent idea, Jason. You're a genius."

Rob and Jason explained the situation to the group.

"Let's find out who did it and make them pay for it," suggested Todd.

"It wasn't me," said Paul Anderson. "I didn't even go to the game last night."

"That's going to take too long," said Melanie. "We have to get him some flowers before his wife's birthday."

"She's right," agreed Jennie. "Let's take up a collection and get him some new plants right away."

"My mom works at a nursery. I can find out how much they cost," offered Mark Mead.

"What if we get him the flowers, and he goes out and gets flowers too?" brought up Matt.

"We could write him a letter of apology and tell him our plans," suggested Mrs. Gray.

"But we didn't do it. Why should we apologize?" asked Tara.

"We'd be apologizing on behalf of the school since we're pretty sure it was somebody from Jerome who did it," answered Mrs. Gray.

"I'll write the letter," offered Lindsay.

"Does everybody agree that this is what we should do?" asked Rob.

"Why don't we take a vote?" suggested Jason.

"That's a good idea," said Mrs. Gray.

There wasn't a single student who voted against the plan.

"When you write the letter, Lindsay, ask Mr. Amopolous if he would like us to do the yard work, or if he would rather do it himself," said Mrs. Gray.

"I think this is a good idea and everything," said Tara, "but it may be a big waste of time. What if we get his yard all planted, and somebody does the same thing again?"

"That won't happen," said Melanie.

"It could," agreed Mrs. Gray. "The school gets lots of complaints from the neighbors about this type of thing. Apparently it happens all the time."

"Let's make up a survey for the neighbors and ask them if their yards have ever been damaged," said Paul.

"What if we find out that lots of them have had flowers and stuff ruined? Are we gonna have to buy everybody new flowers?" asked Mark.

"We could get the whole school involved. Maybe each homeroom could adopt a house on the block and sort of take care of it," said Jennie.

"That's a great idea!" said Mrs. Gray.

"We'll need to get some kind of flyer out to all of the homerooms," said Jason. "Who has a computer at home?"

"I do," said Todd. "If you tell me what to say, I can work on it tonight."

The students decided to split up into groups. Rob and Jason were co-leaders of the project. They helped each of the groups get coordinated. Lindsay used part of her lunch hour to finish writing the letter, and the whole class met right after school in Mrs. Gray's room so that everyone could sign it. The bus people went first, and Jason and Rob were the last ones to sign it.

They rode straight over to Mr. Amopolous's house with it. He had yanked out the entire bed of violets. The soil was raked and leveled, but it didn't seem as though he had planted any new flowers yet. The yard looked strangely empty even though there were many other plants and shrubs.

"Do you think he's home?" asked Jason.

"I hope so. Let's ring the bell," said Rob.

The boys rang the bell, waited, and rang the bell again.

"He's not home," said Rob, feeling disappointed. "We'll have to leave the letter."

The two boys slipped the letter under his back door and left.

"We can stop by in the morning to make sure he found it," said Jason.

"I feel better already just knowing we're going to try to make it up to him," said Rob.

"Yeah, me too."

©1994 by Incentive Publications, Inc., Nashville, TN.   73

The boys left home a little early the next morning so they could spend some time talking with Mr. Amopolous, but when they got to his house, he was not in his familiar place in the yard, nor did he answer his door

"I hope nothing's wrong," said Rob.

"Where could he be?" asked Jason.

"He could be out buying more flowers and vegetable seeds."

"I doubt it. He should have read our note by now."

"Well, we'll just have to try again after school," said Rob.

That day during Prime Time the students in Mrs. Gray's class went on with their plans. Each student needed to bring in two dollars to buy the violets. Mark and Paul worked together on the flower committee.

"When my mom told the owner of the nursery what we were doing, he offered to sell the plants to us at a discount. If each of you can bring in two dollars, we'll have enough violets for Mr. Amopolous to take to his wife and eight bedding plants to put in his yard," reported Mark. "Paul will tell you all about the violets."

Paul is sort of the class genius. He loves to research ideas, so this assignment was a natural for him. He whipped out his note pad and began reading to the class. "We are going to be purchasing sweet violets. Their scientific name is *viola odorata*. They are very hardy and best known for their fragrance. They are perennials."

"What does that mean?" asked Tara.

"It means they come back year after year. They actually reseed themselves."

"What color are they going to be?" asked Jennie.

"They're available in white, pink, purple, and shades of violet," answered Paul with authority.

"How do we know what colors to buy?" asked Lindsay.

"Mr. Amopolous had shades of violet in his yard, but maybe we should ask him if that's what he wants again?" said Rob.

"Why don't I write you a pass to use the phone, and you can try to call him right now," said Mrs. Gray.

"I don't know his number, but Jason and I could look it up."

Mrs. Gray wrote them passes, and they hurried down to the office to make the call.

"Are you finished with your report, Paul?" asked Mrs. Gray.

"Well, there is one more thing you should know. They grow to be about ten inches high."

"Thank you, Paul. That was an excellent report," complimented Mrs. Gray.

"Is there anything else we need to discuss?" asked Mrs. Gray.

"I have a sample flyer to show the class," said Todd, holding up the flyer.

"Nice graphics, Todd," said Mark.

"Thanks. Do you guys think this will do?" asked Todd.

"I think it's great. I'll help you run them off and deliver them to the home-rooms," offered Tara.

"Are you willing to use part of your lunch hour so we can get them out today?" asked Mrs. Gray.

"I am," answered Todd.

"Me too," said Tara.

"Terrific!" beamed Mrs. Gray. "We're really moving along. Who would like to collect the money?"

Three hands shot up. Mrs. Gray chose Mark and Jennie.

Before they had a chance to collect any money, Rob and Jason returned to class looking very upset.

"Mrs. Amopolous is very sick. Mr. Amopolous is staying with her day and night," said Jason.

"We were lucky to catch him at home. He just came home to change clothes and call his sons. They will be flying in tonight. I never even talked to him about the violets," said Rob.

"We have to work fast," said Paul. "Let's get the violets planted today before his sons get there. We can fix up a bouquet and give it to Mr. Amopolous, and he can give it to his wife."

"How many of you think that's what we should do?" asked Mrs. Gray.

Everyone's hands flew up.

"I can drive over to the nursery and pick up the plants during my lunch hour. How many of you can stay after school tonight?"

Ten students raised their hands.

"That's great. If any of you need phone passes to call home, see me before you leave Prime Time," said Mrs. Gray.

"We're going to need some garden tools," said Mark.

"You're right. Who lives close to school?" asked Mrs. Gray.

"I can go get ours," offered Rob.

"So can I," offered Matt.

"Rob or Jason, do you know the name of the nursing home?" asked Mrs. Gray.

"Yes, it's the same one my grandpa was in," said Rob. Suddenly he felt a flood of emotion overwhelm him as every painful memory of his grandfather's death surfaced. His grandpa had died two years ago, and he had thought it was behind him. The hurt now seemed every bit as painful as it had been two years ago. Not wanting to cry in front of the class, he got up and left the room.

©1994 by Incentive Publications, Inc., Nashville, TN. 75

"Can I go with him?" asked Jason.

"I think he may need a little time to be alone, Jason. Let's give him a few minutes and if he doesn't come back, I'll let you check on him," said Mrs. Gray.

Then she turned to the class and asked, "How many of you have lost a grandparent or someone else really close to you?" Almost half of the class had their hands raised. "Then I'm sure you can understand how Rob is feeling. As we work on this project, it may stir up some feelings you have locked inside of you. Be kind and supportive of one another.

"The bell is about to ring. We'll meet in my room right after school. Oh, and one more thing. I think you're a pretty terrific group of kids for caring so much . . ."

The bell cut her off, and it was just as well because some of the students thought they noticed tears in her eyes.

Mark's mother had set aside some of the most exquisite violets Mrs. Gray had ever seen. She had also fixed up a beautiful bouquet of them at no extra charge. Every shade of violet and purple was represented. Only its fragrance surpassed its beauty.

The students worked diligently in Mr. Amopolous's yard for about an hour. With ten of them working, they were amazed at how much they could accomplish in a short amount of time. While they were there, they watered his yard, swept the walkway, picked up the litter, and pulled a few weeds which had cropped up in the past day or two. They left around 4:30, feeling tired but very proud of their work.

Since Rob's family knew where the nursing home was, he took the bouquet home with him. He promised the group that he would make sure Mr. Amopolous would have it to give to his wife that night.

"I don't know what to say," said Rob.

"You don't have to say much. The flowers will pretty much say it all," said Mrs. Clarke.

Rob asked the receptionist for Mrs. Amopolous's room number and he and his mom started down the hall. She was in room thirty-five. When they got to her room, they found the door closed.

"What should I do?" asked Rob.

"Knock gently."

Rob knocked and waited. Mrs. Clarke slipped back into the lobby. Soon Mr. Amopolous came to the door. He was surprised to find Rob there. He had been expecting his sons.

"Rob, how nice of you to come by," said Mr. Amopolous, stepping out into the hallway so they could talk.

"These are for you to give to Mrs. Amopolous because of what happened to yours," said Rob. "They're from my class at school."

Mr. Amopolous was clearly pleased. "If anything can bring a smile to her face, these will. Thank you, and please tell your friends how much this means to Mrs. Amopolous and me."

"How is Mrs. Amopolous?"

"She's resting comfortably, but the doctors don't think she'll last much longer. She suffered a stroke two days ago. I only hope she can hang on until my sons get here. When she smells these flowers, I know she will have the courage to keep fighting. Now if you'll excuse me, I must get back to Mrs. Amopolous and give her these wonderful violets. Good-bye, my friend."

"Good-bye."

Mrs. Amopolous died two days after she received the violets. She did get to see her sons one last time. A week after her funeral, Mrs. Gray's class received the following letter from Mr. Amopolous.

Dear Friends,

I want to thank you for the beautiful bouquet of violets. I wish you could have seen the look on Mrs. Amopolous's face when she smelled their sweet fragrance. It is a memory I shall treasure for the rest of my life.

Each day as I care for the bed of violets which you so kindly planted for me, I think of my dear wife and my friends at Jerome Middle School. They're your flowers now, and I hope you will enjoy them as you pass my house with your friends. They are truly the sweetest violets I have ever had in my garden.

Your friend,

Mr. Amopolous

SWEET VIOLETS

Overview

Students will be involved in a week of activities focusing on what it means to be a good neighbor.

Day One—Topic: What is a good neighbor?

Project: Students make a Good Neighbor poster.

Day Two—Topic: Being a good neighbor in the classroom

Project: Students complete the People Hunt worksheet (page 79).

Day Three—Topic: Being a good neighbor at school

Project: Campus project (page 80)

Day Four—Topic: Campus project (page 80, continued)

Day Five—Topic: Being a good neighbor in the community

Project: Students complete the community service project (page 81).

Topic One: WHAT IS A GOOD NEIGHBOR?
Time: 25–30 minutes

Small Group Activity

MATERIALS NEEDED:

- paper   • markers, crayons, or colored pencils

DIRECTIONS:

1. Students form groups of no more than four.
2. Each group writes an acrostic describing what it means to be a good neighbor.
3. Encourage students to be creative, but stress that all poems must spell GOOD NEIGHBOR. For example:

Go out of your way to be friendly.
O
O
D

N
E
I
G
H
B
O
R

Topic Two: PEOPLE HUNT

Ask fellow students about neighborly acts they may have done or witnessed and fill in names to complete as many boxes as possible.

(Your name goes here.)	I borrowed paper today.	I helped a teacher this week.
I borrowed a pencil today.	I loaned someone paper today.	A teacher helped me this week.
I loaned someone a pencil today.	I borrowed clothing from a friend this week.	This month I helped a student pick up dropped belongings.
I helped clean up the classroom this week.	I loaned clothing to a friend this week.	This month someone helped me pick up something I dropped.
Someone had to clean up after me in the classroom this week.	I did my part on a group assignment.	I gave a compliment to someone today.
I helped another student with a class assignment today.	Another student helped me with make-up work this month.	Someone complimented me today.
Another student helped me with a class assignment today.	I helped a student find out about make-up work this month.	I smiled and said hello to a teacher today.
Another student called me for help on an assignment this month.	I called another student for help on an assignment this month.	A teacher smiled and said hello to me today.

Topic Three: BEING A GOOD NEIGHBOR AT SCHOOL
Time: Two 25-minute sessions

Large Group Activity

MATERIALS NEEDED:
- stationery for thank-you notes
- appreciation gifts

DIRECTIONS:
Students will recognize school employees and thank them for the parts they play in making the school run smoothly.

1. Students make a list of all school personnel. Include administrators, teachers, bus drivers, custodians, cafeteria workers, etc.

2. Discuss with the students ways to show appreciation for these workers. Suggestions might include a large homemade cookie, a candy bar, a flower, etc.

3. Each student selects one or more employees and writes a thank-you note to that person.

4. Ask for volunteers to bring in baked goods or whatever the class decides upon. Each item should be individually wrapped.

5. Make arrangements to deliver the item and thank-you note to each person.

Topic Four: BEING A GOOD NEIGHBOR IN THE COMMUNITY
Time: 25+ minutes

Small Group Activity

DIRECTIONS:

1. Students form groups of no more than four.

2. Groups brainstorm ideas for a service project for the area near the school. For example, students clean up a shopping area often littered by students or survey neighbors whose yards and homes border the school. Remind students that projects can be as simple as passing out a calendar of school activities or as involved as weekly clean-up of student litter. Allow 5–10 minutes for the brainstorming.

Large Group Activity

DIRECTIONS:

1. Each group reports its ideas to the large group. Appoint a student to keep a listing on a large sheet of paper or use the chalkboard.

2. After a brief discussion, the class votes on one project.

3. Determine resources needed to complete the project.

Checklist

Will you need . . .

_____ money to carry out this project?

_____ permission slips?

_____ after-school time?

_____ address list of school neighbors?

_____ help from people outside your class?

_____ donations—either money or goods?

82

SURPRISE
PARTY

Jennie shut off her alarm clock, opened her big, green eyes, and stretched. Then she threw off her covers and walked across her bedroom into her private bathroom to take a shower. After drying off and carefully hanging up her towel, she opened her closet and quickly grabbed one of her new shirts. Any one would do since she had already decided to wear her white shorts. Before going down to breakfast, she styled her long, dark hair, put on her make-up, and made her bed. She glanced at her room on the way out the door, making sure everything was put away. Her parents expected her room to be immaculately clean at all times.

Meanwhile, Jennie's best friend, Melanie, was getting dressed at her house. She shared a bedroom (and everything else) with her ten-year-old sister Terry.

Melanie stumbled out of bed, tripping over a towel she had left on the floor after her shower the night before. Pounding on the bathroom door at the end of the hall, she shouted, "Tim! Hurry up! It's my turn for the bathroom!"

"O.K., O.K.! I'll be out in a minute." Melanie's older brother, a sophomore, had first dibs on the bathroom because he had to be at school by 7:30 a.m.

"It's about time," complained Melanie as Tim opened the bathroom door.

"I think I understand," teased Tim. "You need all the time you can get to work on that face."

Melanie's face turned bright red with embarrassment, and she slammed the bathroom door without a reply. She was very self-conscious about her complexion. Tim knew better than to tease her about her face, of all things, but the words rolled out of his mouth before he could think.

Melanie quickly brushed her long, blond hair and pulled it back with a band. Grabbing just a few strands of hair, she curled them slightly with her hot curling iron. Next, she teased them to give them some body, and then sprayed them in place. When she got back to her room, she looked at the clock. She had exactly eight minutes left. She opened her closet door and looked over her pitiful wardrobe. There wasn't one thing she wanted to wear. Reluctantly, she decided on her jean shorts and a plain, navy blue T-shirt. Grabbing a piece of toast her mom had left for her and her backpack, she hurried out the door to catch her bus.

When Melanie got off the bus, Jennie was waiting for her at her locker. "Hi."

"Mel, you just missed Rob, Todd, and Jason. They want us to go out with them for pizza after the dance tonight," explained Jennie.

"The dance. I forgot all about it. What am I going to wear? What are you wearing?" asked Melanie.

"I don't know. I haven't thought about it yet. So, what about going with them for pizza?"

"I think we should go. Definitely. Will Matt be there too?"

"Rob didn't mention Matt, but he usually does stuff with those guys."

"What I would give for one slow dance with him," sighed Melanie.

"Does he even know you like him?" asked Jennie.

"I hope not. You're the only one I've told. You haven't told anybody have you?"

"Well . . ."

"Well, what?" asked Melanie, beginning to get upset.

"I think I may have told Lindsay," admitted Jennie. "I'm sure she won't tell anyone."

"You told Lindsay? She tells Tara everything, and Tara tells everybody everything! The whole school probably knows," moaned Melanie.

"Sorry, Mel."

"Are Lindsay and Tara going out with us for pizza?" asked Melanie.

"Probably. I think Rob likes Tara."

"No way. Rob likes you, Jennie."

"We're just good friends. He doesn't really like me, but I kind of wish he did."

"Really?"

"He's so cool. He makes me laugh. I can be totally depressed when I see him, and after a few minutes he's got me cracking up over something."

"Jennie, you better get your books. The bell's going to ring. I'll see you at lunch."

"Bye, Mel."

That one day of school seemed about a week long. Everyone was excited about the dance and their plans for the weekend. The teachers fought a losing battle that day trying to keep the kids' minds on anything related to academics.

Melanie and Jennie got dressed at Jennie's house since Jennie had invited Melanie to spend the night. Melanie loved spending the night there because Jennie didn't have any brothers and sisters to bother them.

"Dad, can you take us to the dance now?"

"Sure. Let me get my keys. You two look awfully pretty tonight."

Both girls blushed.

"What time should I pick you up?"

"We're going to Pete's Pizza right after the dance with a bunch of our friends, so I'll call you when we need a ride."

"How are you getting to the pizza place?"

"Walking."

"Your mom and I are going to a movie. We'll just plan on picking you up at eleven."

"O.K."

"Thanks for the ride, Mr. McCormick."

"You're welcome. Have fun girls. Try not to break too many hearts tonight."

"Dad! You are so corny. Bye. Thanks for driving us."

Jennie and Melanie showed their I.D.'s, paid their money, and looked around for their friends.

"There they are," shouted Jennie above the loud music. "Look, Matt's with them."

"How do I look? Maybe I shouldn't have worn your white jeans. They make me look fat."

"They do not! You look great. Stop worrying," advised Jennie.

"They're coming over here. Matt looks so good I can hardly stand it!"

"He never went to any dances last year. I think this is his first one ever. I wonder if he can dance?" asked Jennie.

"I'd be glad to teach him," volunteered Melanie.

"Matt, you ask Jennie, and I'll ask Melanie," said Todd.

"What if she says no?" worried Matt.

"She won't."

"O.K. If you say so. Personally, I think coming to this dance was the biggest mistake of my life."

"Why? I thought you really liked Jennie."

"I do. That's why I don't want to make a complete fool of myself in front of her," said Matt, getting more nervous with each step he took.

"Relax, Matt."

"Aren't you nervous? Aren't you afraid Melanie will say no?"

"Naw. She's too nice."

"Hi, Jennie. Do you want to dance?" asked Matt, his big, gorgeous, blue eyes looking right into hers.

Jennie glanced over at Melanie. She was really taken by surprise. This wasn't how it was supposed to go at all. She couldn't make eye contact with Melanie because Todd was talking to her.

Finally, she answered. "Sure, I'd like to Matt."

The two of them walked to the dance floor just as the D. J. put on a slow song. Matt took Jennie in his arms, and Jennie forgot all about Rob and Melanie and the rest of the world. She didn't even notice Todd and Melanie who were dancing right next to them. Unfortunately, Melanie was very much aware of Matt and Jennie. She was dancing with Todd, but her mind was on Matt and Jennie.

When the music stopped, Melanie thanked Todd and went back over to the group and waited for Jennie to return. But the D.J. put on another song, and Matt and Jennie danced again. Melanie hung around with the rest of the group and tried to pretend that she didn't care that Jennie was with Matt.

"I can't believe Jennie is dancing with Matt again. I thought you liked him," said Tara.

"Oh, I used to for a while, but not anymore," lied Melanie.

"Then why do you look like that?" asked Tara.

"Like what?"

"Like you just lost your best friend."

"Maybe I have," answered Melanie. Then she walked off to the girls' bathroom.

Jennie asked anxiously, "Where's Melanie?"

"She's in the bathroom," answered Tara.

As usual, the bathroom was crowded with girls fixing their make-up, combing their hair, talking about boys, avoiding boys, and a few of them actually had to use the facilities.

"Mel? Where are you?" yelled Jennie. Then she spotted her making small talk with Michelle Wyse, a girl Melanie normally wouldn't be caught dead talking to. It was then that she knew for sure that Melanie must really be mad at her.

"Hey, Mel, can I talk to you?"

Melanie and Jennie had been best friends since fifth grade. They rarely got mad at each other, so when they did it was a very unfamiliar and painful feeling for both of them.

Melanie looked at Jennie and felt her hurt feelings well up inside of her. "Jen, how could you dance with him?"

"I'm sorry, Mel. He caught me completely off guard. I didn't know what to do, so I said yes. Once we were out on the dance floor, I just felt like I was melting in his arms. He looked at me with those eyes of his . . ."

"Spare me the details, Jen!"

"I'm sorry. I wish it had been you he asked and not me. Honest, I do."

"Right."

"I promise I'll never dance with him again."

Melanie stood there for a while trying to blink back her tears. "Jen, it's O.K. I want you to dance with him. I can't force him to like me."

Jennie knew how hard this must be for Melanie to admit. "Thanks for understanding, Mel."

"Let's go back out there," said Melanie.

"Oh, one more thing. You know how we're supposed to go to Pete's Pizza later? Well, Matt invited us to a party at his house instead. Do you want to go?"

"Who's going to be there?"

"Everybody."

"What about your dad? He's picking us up at the pizza place."

"Oh, yeah. Huh. I forgot."

"Matt lives just a couple of blocks away from here. We could leave the party in time to walk over to Pete's Pizza by eleven o'clock," suggested Melanie.

"That's a great idea, Mel. You're brilliant."

The dance ended at nine o'clock, and the students from Jerome Middle School scattered in all directions. Some went for pizza, others were picked up by their parents, and some went on to parties. Jennie, Melanie, Tara, Lindsay, Rob, Jason, Todd, and Matt walked over to Matt's house en masse. Matt held Jennie's hand the whole way.

All of the lights were out when they got to Matt's house.

"Wait a second while I get the key," said Matt. Like most families, Matt's parents hid a key for the kids to use if they were ever locked out. Matt moved a small flower pot on the front patio, picked up the key, and opened the door.

"Where are his parents?" whispered Melanie.

"I don't know. He didn't tell me they wouldn't be home. They're probably at a movie or something and will be home any minute," offered Jennie.

"Put on some music and let's party!" said Jason.

"My parents would ground me forever if they knew I was at a party with no adults," said Jennie.

"Mine too," agreed Melanie.

"Well, let's just stay a little while. We can walk over to Pete's Pizza and wait for my parents."

"Good thinking, Jen."

"Matt, do you have anything to drink?" asked Lindsay.

"Yeah, there's some soda in the refrigerator, but we can't drink too much or my parents will notice."

"O.K. We'll share," said Tara.

"Crank the music, Todd. I like this song," shouted Rob.

"Let's order some pizza," suggested Matt.

"Good idea, Matt. I'm starving," admitted Jennie.

"Matt, I think somebody's here," screamed Todd over the loud music.

Matt looked puzzled, but he went to the door and opened it. Much to his dismay, there were two car loads of high school kids at his door. He didn't know any of them except for Bill Barton, who lived on his block.

"Hey, Matt, how's it going, buddy?" asked Bill. "We thought we heard a party. We were just cruisin' the neighborhood."

"Bill, you guys have to leave. My parents aren't home and . . . "

"Relax, little buddy. We'll just stay for a few minutes," coaxed Bill, pushing himself through the door. Nine others followed him.

"They're not even in high school, Bill. Let's go," said one of the girls. Unfortunately, Bill had been drinking, so he was feeling no pain and making no sense.

"O.K., but I need to use the john first," said Bill, slurring his words and setting his beer can down on the coffee table.

Matt was beginning to feel distressed. He wanted these kids out of his house. He soon got his wish for there was a knock at the door. This time it was the police. The neighbor across the street had called them when she heard the noise and saw the cars parked in front of the house. Mrs. Morris had asked her to keep an eye on the house while she and her husband were away. Matt was staying with Todd while they were gone.

Todd turned down the music, Rob hid the beer can behind the couch, and Jason headed down the hall to make sure Bill stayed in the bathroom.

"Good evening. Is there an adult on the premises?"

"No, sir, but this is my house," Matt spoke up, sounding as respectful and polite as he could.

"Is everything alright here? We received a call from your neighbor that something may be wrong at this address. According to her, she's been asked to watch the house," explained the officer.

"Well, we were just leaving for Pete's Pizza. My neighbor and some of his friends just stopped in to use our bathroom. They'll be leaving right away."

The officer looked around the room. No one seemed to be out of control, so the officer bid them good night and left.

"That was a close one," said Rob.

"Let's get out of here," added Tara and Lindsay in unison.

"What about Bill? He's passed out in the bathroom," Jason informed the group.

"Oh, that's just great!"

"Don't worry," said one of the boys who had come in with Bill. "We'll get him to the car, and I'll drive him home. I haven't been drinking."

It took them about ten minutes to get Bill to his car. He was a big guy, and it took three of them to get him on his feet. He shuffled along to the car with their assistance.

Jennie looked at her watch. She and Melanie had exactly fifteen minutes to get to Pete's Pizza.

"We have to leave right now. Jennie's parents are picking us up at Pete's Pizza at eleven o'clock."

"My parents are, too," said Rob.

"Mine, too," added Tara.

Matt locked up the house, put away the key, and the group hurried down the street toward the pizza parlor.

"I'm going to have fun this weekend because when my parents get back from their trip they're going to kill me," said Matt.

"Maybe your neighbor won't say anything," added Jennie.

"Not a chance. She'll probably make it sound like half the school was at my house."

"Why don't you go over there tomorrow and offer to mow her lawn or something? You have a couple of days to show her what a nice, thoughtful, responsible young man you are," joked Rob.

"You should do something wonderful for your parents before they get home. Like clean the garage or clean your room," advised Melanie. "That always works with my parents."

"I think he should party the whole weekend while he's got the chance," said Jason. "There's plenty of time to clean the garage when he's grounded."

"If we don't start walking a little faster we may all be grounded. It's almost eleven. My parents think I've been at Pete's Pizza this whole time," said Rob.

"Same here," agreed Lindsay.

The whole group spontaneously began to run. They arrived at Pete's slightly out of breath and a couple of minutes late. As luck would have it, their parents were not late.

"My mom is late to everything," said Todd. "Why couldn't she have been late picking us up tonight?"

"My parents are so unreasonable," complained Matt.

"What happened? Did your neighbor tell on you?" asked Rob.

"Yes. I knew she would. Adults always stick together on this type of thing."

"I know. My mom wouldn't feel right if she let even one kid on our block get away with something."

"Are you grounded?"

"For two weeks. I'd like to get my hands on Bill Barton. It's all his fault. Mrs. Johnson never would have noticed just us. We weren't making that much noise. It was the cars in front of the house that tipped her off."

"Too bad Bill Barton weighs about 180 pounds and plays football," said Rob.

"Yeah, I guess he can pretty much do whatever he wants and get away with it. Did you get in trouble?"

"Not really. At least I didn't get grounded. My parents have this probation thing they do with us. If they catch me not being where I said I was going in the next month, I'm grounded for two weeks. Of course they don't know that your parents weren't home or that the police came over. I forgot to mention those trivial details. What happened to Todd? Your mom told his mom about everything, didn't she?"

"Yeah, they're good friends. They talk about everything, which is a real hassle sometimes."

"So, is Todd grounded?"

"That's a dumb question. Of course. He and I got the same punishment, except his mom usually weakens and lets him off after about a week. My parents are so mad, I'll be lucky if they don't decide to make it three weeks."

"Well, I have to go, Matt. My sister wants to use the phone."

"I need to go, too. I'm not supposed to be on the phone," said Matt.

"Your parents were so understanding last night. My parents have a real thing about me being exactly where I tell them I'm going," said Melanie.

"I've never really gotten in trouble for anything, so they trust me. I always tell them the truth. I just do," explained Jennie.

"You make it sound easy. I don't really lie to my parents, but sometimes I don't tell them everything. It makes me feel more like I'm in charge of my life. I'm not a little kid anymore, and I like my privacy. But my parents, especially my mom, want to know everything I do and say."

"I guess my parents are like that too, but I don't know, I guess we're just so close that I'm used to it. It does have its advantages. They let me do almost anything I want because they trust me," said Jennie.

"Is that why you told them everything—even about Matt's parents not being home and about that drunk guy?"

"None of that stuff was our fault. I mean, I should have asked Matt if his parents would be home, but I just assumed they would be. Next time I'll ask."

"You'll sound like a big baby if you do," warned Melanie.

"You're right," admitted Jennie.

"I liked that his parents were gone. That is, I liked it until Beer Breath Bill and his friends showed up."

"Did you really? I just kept thinking that my parents wouldn't like it if they knew the party were unchaperoned, and I felt uncomfortable the whole time."

"You're such a goody-goody," Melanie teased.

"Look, somebody's got to keep you out of trouble," said Jennie, teasing back.

"Let's call Tara and Lindsay and see if they got in trouble," suggested Melanie.

"They're at Tara's. Lindsay spent the night," said Jennie. "You call them while I take my shower."

"O.K."

"Hi, Tara? What are you doing?"

"Nothing. Lindsay and I are thinking about going to the mall," answered Tara.

"Then I take it you guys didn't get into trouble last night."

"No, not at all. I just made it sound like we finished our pizza early so we went for a little walk. My mom didn't think anything of it."

"What happened with you guys?" asked Tara.

"Nothing, really. Jennie just told her parents what happened and we got a little lecture about using good judgment, but that was it."

"Did Jennie tell her everything—even about the cops and that drunk guy?"

"Yep."

"Amazing—also not too bright. My mom goes to an aerobics class with her mom. I hope they don't get to talking about the dance," said Tara, feeling slightly uneasy about the situation.

"Well, how was she supposed to know you were going to make up that story to tell your mom?" said Melanie in Jennie's defense.

"It's not like I wanted to make up that story. It's just that it's too risky for me to tell my parents stuff like that. Sometimes they're cool, but sometimes they freak out on me. I didn't want to take a chance on getting grounded for the weekend," explained Tara.

"I know what you mean. My parents are the same way. I just hope your mom doesn't find out from Mrs. McCormick."

"You and me both!"

"You're not mad at Jennie, are you?"

"No. It's not her fault she can be so honest with her parents," laughed Tara.

"Well, I have to go. Jennie's out of the shower. We'll call you guys if we decide to go to the mall."

"O.K. Bye."

"Bye."

Melanie hung up the phone and told Jennie about her conversation with Tara.

"I think Tara should tell her mom what really happened because I just know my mom is going to say something about it to her mom. My mom leads such a boring, ordinary life that anything involving the cops and drinking is exciting," said Jennie.

"She's afraid she'll get grounded."

"Well, she could tell her Sunday night. Our moms don't have aerobics class until Monday night. Is she mad at me?"

"Naw, you know Tara. She doesn't get mad at anybody."

"What are you going to tell your parents when you go home?" asked Jennie.

"I don't know. If I talk a lot about the dance, my parents won't ask me anything about the rest of the night."

"What if they do?"

"Look, Jen, my parents have three kids, and they both work. They don't have time to ask me all those questions. It's one of the few benefits of having brothers and sisters."

"Well, I guess I'll just have to make sure you don't get into too much trouble."

"Jennie, I've got an idea for tonight. If you can spend the night at my house, maybe we can sneak out and meet Matt, Rob, and Jas . . . "

"WHAT? Do you know how much trouble we'll be in if your par . . . "

Jennie quit yelling when she saw Melanie laughing.

"GOTCHA!"

"I knew you were only kidding," said Jennie, trying to save face.

"Right," said Melanie. "Of course you did."

Topic One: FRIENDSHIP
Time: 25–30 minutes

Large Group Discussion

MATERIALS NEEDED:

- discussion questions (listed below)

DIRECTIONS:

Introduce the following questions in a large group discussion about friendship.

1. What did Melanie do when Matt asked Jennie to dance? How did she feel?
2. Why did Jennie look for Melanie after she finished dancing with Matt?
3. How did Melanie and Jennie work out their problem?

Small Group Game

MATERIALS NEEDED:

- Friendzee game sheet for each student (page 94)
- one die for each group of four

DIRECTIONS:

1. The students form groups of no more than four.
2. Give each student a game sheet.
3. Give each group one die.
4. Begin play with the student whose birthday falls closest to today's date.
5. Player rolls the die and responds to the instructions associated with that number. For example, when a student rolls a one, he or she must name three characteristics of a good friend.
6. Player marks #1 on his or her Friendzee game sheet.
7. Play proceeds clockwise around the table. A player who rolls a number already marked off passes to the next player.
8. The object of the game is to be the first player to mark all six numbers.

FRIENDZEE GAME SHEET

1. Name three characteristics of a good friend.

2. Describe how you and a good friend met.

3. Share how you make up with a friend after you have had a fight.

4. In what way do you act differently around an old friend than you do around a new friend?

5. Name one reason why people stop being friends.

6. Share a time when a friend betrayed your trust or a time when you betrayed a friend's trust. How did you feel?

No repeat answers allowed!

Topic Two: **TRUST**
Time: 25–30 minutes

Self-assessment: Can You Be Trusted?

MATERIALS NEEDED:

- assessment form (page 96)
- one sheet of butcher paper
- permanent marker

DIRECTIONS:

1. Begin the activity by asking each student to complete a copy of the assessment form.

2. Encourage students to select one statement where they scored themselves as untrustworthy.

3. Students will agree to work on building trust in this area for one month.

4. Have each student write down his or her statement on a sheet of paper. This paper should then be stapled or placed in an envelope for privacy. Place the envelope in the student's personal folder to be evaluated by the student in one month.

5. On a large sheet of butcher paper, write "TRUST IS . . ." with a permanent marker. Invite every student to finish the sentence. Post this in the room to remind students of their agreement to work on building trust.

CAN YOU BE TRUSTED?

DIRECTIONS:

Read each statement. Write down the number that best describes you.

UNTRUSTWORTHY   **TRUSTWORTHY**

1   2   3   4   5

Can you be trusted to:

_____ come home on time?

_____ keep a secret?

_____ tell your parents where you are really spending the night?

_____ be where you said you would be?

_____ leave a party if there is drinking?

_____ take care of clothing you've borrowed from a friend?

_____ take care of clothing you've borrowed from a family member?

_____ call an adult when you need help?

_____ tell the truth even when it may get you in trouble?

_____ tell the truth when it may get a friend in trouble?

_____ baby-sit and care for younger children?

Are you trusting enough to:

_____ tell a friend a secret?

_____ lend your favorite shirt to a friend?

_____ share your feelings with a small group of students?

_____ share your feelings with an adult?

_____ depend on your friends to do what they say?

──Topic Three: **TRUST/JEALOUSY/FRIENDSHIP**─

Time: 25–30 minutes

Small Group Discussion and Writing Activity

MATERIALS NEEDED:

- "Dear Abby" letters (pages 98 and 99, cut one slip for each group)
- pencil and paper

DIRECTIONS:

1. The students form groups of no more than four people.
2. Each group receives a "Dear Abby" letter to read and discuss.
3. Group members collaborate and write a response to the letter.
4. One member from each small group will share the group's "Dear Abby" letter with the large group.
5. Another group member will then read the group's letter of advice.

Follow-up Activity

Have the students write anonymous letters to "Dear Abby" and submit them to the class for small group discussion and advice.

"DEAR ABBY" LETTERS

Dear Abby,

I really need your advice. I am thirteen years old, and my parents won't let me go anywhere without checking up on me. Two months ago I lied to them about where I was going, and ever since then, they treat me like a child. How can I win back their trust?

Signed,

Not To Be Trusted

Dear Abby,

All of my friends are going to a concert in three weeks. My parents won't allow me to go to concerts unless there is an adult there. (I'm thirteen years old.) I've already purchased a ticket, and I really want to go. I'm thinking of telling my parents that I'm going to a movie and then spending the night with a friend, but I'm afraid they may find out the truth and ground me forever. What should I do?

Signed,

Doomed

Dear Abby,

I'm in eighth grade, and I have a problem. I'm very jealous of my friends. They all seem to get picked for everything. Two of them are in student council, the other three play on the basketball team, and I'm feeling really left out and jealous. My feelings are getting in the way of our friendship. What should I do?

Signed,

A Real Loser

Dear Abby,

I'm thirteen years old, and I really need your help. I have been best friends with "Terry" since fourth grade. We do everything together, but lately "Terry" has been spending a lot of time with a new kid who just moved to our school. I'm afraid I'm losing "Terry" as my best friend. What should I do?

Signed,

Worried

— "DEAR ABBY" LETTERS —

Dear Abby,

My best friend has lots of brothers and sisters. I am an only child. Whenever I spend the day at "Pat's" house, I feel jealous when I go home to my empty house. I'm usually happy, but I feel so miserable when I think of what "Pat" has and what I'm missing. What can I do about these feelings? Help!

Signed,

Unhappy Now

Dear Abby,

I'm in junior high, and I like a guy who's in high school. He wants to take me out on a date, but my parents won't let me go out with him. I don't want to get in trouble with my parents, but I really like this guy, and I don't think I can resist the temptation to sneak out on a date with him much longer. Help!

Signed,

In Love

Dear Abby,

My friend and I like to trade clothes. The problem is that he has lots of nice clothes and I have only a few. I take good care of mine because I know they have to last a long time. My friend is not careful with my clothes. My clothes are often stained and dirty when he returns them. What should I do?

Signed,

Frustrated

Dear Abby,

I really need your help. I think a good friend of mine stole some money from me. I'm afraid that I will lose "Chris" as my friend if I confront "Chris" about this. I've tried to just forget about it, but every time I'm with "Chris" I feel like I have to keep my stuff under lock and key. What should I do?

Signed,

Suspicious Friend

PARENTS ARE IMPOSSIBLE

Tara grabbed her notebook, slammed her locker, and hurried to class without speaking to anyone.

"What's the matter with her?" asked Melanie.

"She's in a bad mood," answered Lindsay.

"Why?"

"Her mom grounded her for no reason at all."

"What happened?"

"She was supposed to come straight home from school yesterday to baby-sit her little sister so her mom could get a haircut. She forgot all about it, and came home on my bus with me so we could work on our lab report for science."

"Couldn't her mom just take Carrie with her?" asked Melanie.

"That's exactly what her mom did, but Carrie acted like a little monster, and now Tara's in trouble."

"That's so unfair," said Melanie.

"I know. Then she and her mom got in a big fight over it because her little sister always gets away with murder, and Tara's sick of it."

"Same with my little sister," agreed Melanie.

"I have to go find Tara. See you later, Mel," called Lindsay.

"Bye."

Lindsay could hear Tara as she approached the doorway to the science classroom.

"Don't try to help me, don't come near me. You've done enough already!"

Judging from the looks of things, Todd had accidentally knocked Tara's notebook off her desk. Her papers were littered across the floor.

"Somebody got up on the . . . "

"Shut up, Todd!"

"Todd, if I were you, I'd give it up and go sit down. Trust me on this one," advised Lindsay, bending down to help her best friend.

"Tara, I hate to tell you this, but I think you grabbed the wrong notebook. This one doesn't have our lab stuff in it, does it?"

"No, it's in my other notebook. I think it's in my locker, unless I left it at home."

"You left it at home?"

"I don't know. I can't remember!"

"I'll finish picking this stuff up. You go ask Mr. Fenwick for a hall pass."

"Mr. Fenwick, I grabbed the wrong notebook by accident. Can I have a pass to go to my locker?"

"Sorry, Tara, the administration has been complaining that there are far too many students out in the halls during class time."

"But it has Lindsay's and my lab report in it," explained Tara.

"I'm afraid you'll have to turn it in late."

"For a lower grade?"

"You know my policy on late work."

"But it's all finished. We even typed it on Lindsay's computer."

"If you've done a good job on it, you can still earn a B," said Mr. Fenwick.

Tara walked back to her desk without saying another word. She knew she was just about to lose it. "That stupid lab report!" she thought.

"Hey, Tara, lighten up. It's only a lab report," said Rob, trying to get a smile out of Tara. "If it makes you feel any better, Jason and I forgot ours at home, too," admitted Rob.

"Forgot to do it, you mean," said Tara.

"Yeah, well, it's almost the same thing. So why are you in such a bad mood? I heard you were grounded," said Rob

"So, what if I am? It's none of your business," snapped Tara.

"Is that what's bothering you? I've been grounded half my life. It gives one a chance to do a lot of self-reflecting. Personally, I always come away from a grounding a new man," said Rob, using his most intellectual voice.

That brought a little bit of a smile to her face.

"That's better. Now we need to work on your plan," advised Rob.

"What plan?"

"The plan that's going to get you ungrounded."

"Nothing will get me ungrounded," answered Tara, feeling depressed again. "I had a big fight with my mom, and if I say anything more she's going to double my grounding."

"Who said anything about talking to your mom? Of course that's out of the question. Parents are completely unreasonable about these things. You have to know what you're doing and treat the situation very delicately," said Rob.

"Rob, you're too much. I don't have a clue what you're talking about."

"Meet me at lunch, and I'll explain everything. In the meantime, try not to trip over your lip!"

Rob and Tara met at the group's usual spot right after lunch. They weren't alone. Lindsay, Jason, Todd, Mark, Matt, Melanie, and Jennie were there too.

"First of all, tonight you've got to mope around the house and be miserable. Don't whine, just look like you're suffering. Be polite to your parents and little sister, but not overly friendly."

"That should be easy," said Tara.

"Tomorrow you start phase two."

Rob made it sound like a war or some community building project.

"Is your room clean?"

"Yea, it's pretty clean."

"Oh, that's too bad. See, I always clean my room to get on my mom's good side. Just come home from school and start cleaning something. Work really hard and make sure it's something your mom will notice."

"My mom will never fall for this, Rob. She'll see right through to what I'm doing. I've tried stuff like this before. She always says, 'Don't think I'm going to let you off the hook just because you're being nice now. It's too late'."

"Her mom is like that," agreed Lindsay.

"Exactly how long are you grounded?" asked Todd.

"For two weeks."

"Did your sister get punished at all?" asked Jennie.

"No, she just got yelled at a little. According to my mom, she was behaving like most four-year-olds would. I know lots of four-year-olds who would have just sat there and colored or something."

"So, mostly you got grounded for forgetting to come straight home?" asked Rob for clarification.

"Yeah, it started with that, and then I got mad and said a few things I shouldn't have."

"Like what?" asked Jason.

"Like I'm sick of being used as her personal baby-sitter whenever she wants me."

"What else?"

"Like I have a life of my own and things I need to do with my free time."

"Anything else?" pressed Rob.

"You sound like a lawyer, Rob," laughed Melanie.

"Don't distract my client," said Rob. "Think."

"I said I hated my sister. And, uh, one last thing. I insulted my mom's new haircut."

"Oh, bad decision," said the group in chorus.

"Pretty dumb, huh? I sort of lost my temper after she grounded me."

"Well, now that I know the facts, I think I can get you off by Christmas," teased Rob. "You know, you weren't doing too badly until that bit about your mom's hair."

"I knew it was hopeless," said Tara.

"It's not hopeless. You've got three behavior problems here. You were irresponsible, selfish, and nasty."

"Thanks a lot, Rob."

"Don't get offended. Personally, I'm proud of you, but we've got to think like a parent."

"Tara, you should buy yourself one of those assignment notebooks like Mrs. Phillips is always telling us to buy. You could write down all of your chores and homework and stuff and show your mom just how responsible you can be," said Melanie.

"Excellent idea," said Rob.

"Should I get a pocket protector, too?" asked Tara. "Only teacher's pets use those assignment books."

"I use one," said Jennie.

"Sorry, Jennie, no offense," apologized Tara.

"It's O.K. It does work, and I keep it in my notebook so nobody really sees it."

"That's true. I didn't even know she had it," said Melanie. "So where are you hiding the pocket protectors?"

"Are they designer brands like the rest of your clothes?" asked Lindsay, joining in on the teasing.

"Very funny," said Jennie.

"Don't hold it against her," said Rob. "She can't help it if she's perfect. That takes care of the irresponsible part. Now for the selfish problem."

"She could offer to baby-sit."

"Too obvious," decided Rob. "Unless there's an obvious need. Then baby-sit and do a great job. Make sure your sister has the time of her life. Let her use your make-up or something."

"I think I'd rather stay grounded."

"Do we have an attitude problem here?" asked Jason.

"What about the haircut remark?" asked Tara. "How am I going to fix that?"

"What did you say about her hair?" asked Matt.

"I don't remember exactly, but it was something like it made her look like a frumpy middle-aged housewife."

"Remind me never to get on your wrong side," teased Mark.

"Is it true?" asked Rob.

"What's that got to do with anything?" asked Tara.

"If it's true, you're dead. Every time she looks in the mirror, she's thinking about what you said."

"Does your dad like the haircut?" asked Melanie.

"He hasn't seen it yet. He's been out of town on a business trip."

"Well, he's your one hope. You've got to get to him before he sees your mom and make sure he notices and gives her a big compliment. Then you can agree and tell your mom that of course you didn't mean what you said. That you were mad and stuff like that," said Rob.

"He's right," agreed Lindsay.

"Look, the bell must have rung. Everybody's going to class," said Matt.

"One last thing, Tara. Parents are always looking for a change in attitude and behavior. Those are the two biggies. Keep them in mind all week, and you'll have it made."

"Thanks a lot you guys," said Tara.

Then they all hurried off to their next class.

"Great, I haven't been to the bathroom yet, and I have Mr. Fenwick next," moaned Melanie. "He's not letting anybody out of class these days."

Tara tried to remember everybody's advice, and for the next couple of days she was a model human being. She found out that her friends were right about everything. Her parents especially liked the assignment notebook. Her dad got his appointment book out and showed her how he organized his week. Thankfully, her mom's hair actually looked pretty good, and she was able to honestly pay her several compliments. Her mom asked her twice to baby-sit for Carrie, and she played with her the whole time her parents were gone. By the end of the week, she practically had her parents wrapped around her little finger. On Thursday night, she overheard them talking in the living room.

"Tara has been awfully sweet lately," said Mr. Johnson. "She sure likes your new haircut. Every time you walk in the room she compliments you. It is a very becoming style."

"Thank you, dear. I'm not sure Tara really means it. She's trying to make up for something rather mean she said about my hair when we were fighting."

"What did she say?"

"I'd rather not repeat it. It was said in anger, and I'd like to keep it between the two of us."

"Do you think you should lift the grounding?"

"I don't know. She's been invited to a slumber party this weekend, and I know that's what she's hoping for."

"Has she asked you about it?"

"No, not yet. Maybe I was a little too hard on her. I do expect her to baby-sit a lot for me."

"There's nothing wrong with her helping out around here."

"I agree, but I think I was taking her for granted a little bit. Now that she's getting older, she does have a lot of things going on in her life."

"True, but you do need to be able to depend on her. It's not easy for you running a business at home and raising Carrie. Tara has to help out."

"I think I'll have a talk with her later tonight and tell her she can go to Lindsay's party. It's awfully important to her."

Tara ran straight back to her room to make sure it was clean when her mother came in to talk to her. She put the assignment notebook out on her desk and started on her homework. Soon she heard a knock on her door.

"Come in. Oh, hi, Mom. Your hair looks . . . "

"Tara, please quit telling me my hair looks good. I know you didn't mean what you said the other day, at least I hope you didn't."

"I didn't, Mom, honest. I was just mad. I'm sorry."

"I've noticed a big change in your behavior and attitude this week."

Tara could hardly keep a straight face when her mother said that, but she had too much at stake to blow it now.

"I've been trying to do better, Mom."

"I feel like we've had the old Tara back these past few days. If you promise to continue being helpful, polite, and responsible, I'll unground you," said Mrs. Johnson, looking at one very happy daughter.

"Thank you, Mom, I promise."

107

"And I promise not to take you for granted as a baby-sitter for Carrie from now on. I'm still going to need your help, but I'll try to do some trading with other moms or something."

Tara got up and gave her mom a big hug. Things turned out better than she ever expected. Naturally, the first thing she did was call Lindsay.

"I'm not grounded anymore!" squealed Tara.

"Does that mean you can come to my party?" asked Lindsay.

"Yeah, I think that's why they let me off for the weekend. I owe it all to Rob and the rest of you guys. Rob should write an instruction manual for teenagers. He could call it *How To Manage Difficult Parents*," said Tara.

Lindsay just started laughing.

"What's so funny?" asked Tara.

"Right before you called I was talking to Jennie who just finished talking to Jason. Guess who just got grounded?"

"Not Rob," said Tara.

"Yes, Rob," said Lindsay.

"Well, I just hope he can come up with a good plan," said Tara.

Topic One: **CONFLICT**
Time: 25–30 minutes

Small Group Brainstorming Session

MATERIALS NEEDED:

- large sheets of butcher paper
- permanent markers

DIRECTIONS:

1. The students form groups of no more than four.

2. Each group will be given one of the following situations to brainstorm (5–7 minutes):

> sibling/sibling conflict
>
> teen/teen conflict
>
> teen/parent conflict
>
> teen/teacher conflict
>
> teen/adult authority figure conflict
>
> adult/adult conflict (issues involving teens)

3. One person lists the conflicts on the butcher paper as the group brainstorms.

4. Next, each group shares the list with the entire class.

5. Save each list for the following day's activity.

Topic Two: CONFLICT
Time: 25–30 minutes

Large Group Activity
Cut and Paste Improvisation Cards

MATERIALS NEEDED:
- classroom set of scissors
- disposable magazines (Sunday magazine sale pamphlets work well)
- seven 3" x 5" index cards (or construction paper cut to size) **per student**
- glue

DIRECTIONS:
1. Each student should cut out pictures of the following:
   - teens (3)
   - adults (2)
   - children (1)
   - objects (1)

   (Note: Use posters from Topic One to remind students that various adult figures are needed. One of the adult cards should be labeled an authority figure. Choose objects that represent a variety of categories, such as animals, clothing, vehicles, telephones, books, notebooks, make-up, jewelry, etc.)

2. Glue the pictures on the cards.
3. Cards should be collected according to category for use with the following day's activity.

Topic Three: CONFLICT
Time: 25–30 minutes

Solving Conflict Through Improvisation

MATERIALS NEEDED:

- posters from Topic One
- improvisation cards from Topic Two

DIRECTIONS:

1. Begin the activity with students working in pairs.
2. Each student draws one card from the person pile and pretends to be that character.
3. One student from each pair also selects an object card.
4. Allow students five minutes to determine a conflict situation involving both players and the object card.
5. Players present and resolve their situation using spontaneous role play.
6. Play continues until the conflict is resolved or the teacher gives the pair a signal to conclude within one minute.

HAVING TROUBLE GETTING STARTED?

Let's say one player has drawn a teacher from the adult card pile. The other player draws a teen card. The object drawn is a telephone. The teacher may accuse the student of making prank calls during lunch using a school phone.

or

The teacher may call the student's home.

HAVING TROUBLE CONCLUDING?

If the students don't know when to sit down, the teacher signals to the pair that they have one minute to conclude.

VARIATION:

Use groups of three or more students to create more complex situations.

DEEP
CREEK

The blue van pulled into the small, primitive parking area. Mrs. Clarke, who had volunteered to drive one group of kids, stopped the car, and Rob, Jason, Matt, and Todd climbed out of the van. Mrs. Phillips, their adult sponsor, pulled in right behind her. She drove a station wagon, which wasn't exactly the neatest looking vehicle, but it did have a cellular phone, which somewhat elevated its status. Melanie, Jennie, Tara, and Lindsay jumped out immediately. The eight students unloaded the camping gear from Mrs. Clarke's van. She said she'd rather make the trip to Deep Creek twice than have to spend the night in a tent. For once, Rob was actually glad that his mom hated camping. As she drove off, Rob waved good-bye and joined his friends in their feeling of delight at being parent-free for the weekend.

"What is that?" asked Melanie, pointing to a rectangular-shaped building.

"It looks like a cabin," said Rob.

The inquisitive group of students quickly hiked up the trail to explore the cabin. The kids didn't know anything of the history of the cabin, but it was obviously quite old. Someone long ago had painted it green, but its boards were now peeling, having weathered badly with time. All of the windows were boarded up, and the door was locked. A very thick chain across the latch was tightly secured with an enormous padlock. Curiously, the screened porch just outside the front door had been left open. A primitive wooden table with heavy, handmade benches was the sole piece of furniture in the otherwise vacant space.

"I wish we could look inside," said Rob.

"We aren't supposed to go near this cabin," explained Mrs. Phillips. "When Mr. Carver willed this land to our school district for outdoor education, he hadn't used this cabin for years. Our district doesn't have the money it would take to refurbish it, so they boarded it up. I don't remember seeing that padlock before, though."

"Maybe someone tried to break into it," said Jennie.

"You may be right," said Mrs. Phillips. "Anyway, you are all to stay away from this cabin. It's not a safe structure."

Mrs. Phillips was in charge of the new Outdoor Education Program at Jerome Middle School. She had an exciting year of trips planned for the students. However, since she had no previous experience running a program of this nature, she selected a group of eight students to take on a trial run.

"Where are we going to set up camp?" asked Lindsay.

"We'll be camping on the other side of Deep Creek. We have to take the trail past this cabin and follow it to the bridge. We'll cross the bridge and camp in the clearing next to the creek. It's a beautiful spot!"

"How far is it?" asked Jennie.

"About a mile," answered Mrs. Phillips.

"I hope it's not uphill. This pack is killing me," complained Melanie.

"You girls are such babies," teased Jason.

"We'll beat you boys there," yelled Tara, not letting Jason get the best of her.

Jennie, Melanie, and Lindsay joined her in setting a brisk pace. Accepting the challenge, Rob, Jason, Matt, and Todd picked up their packs and set off down the trail. Mrs. Phillips grabbed her pack and hoped that the aerobics class she had been taking had gotten her in good enough shape to keep up with her more than energetic students.

All eight students reached the bridge without any signs of tiring, so they crossed the bridge together with Mrs. Phillips following not too far behind them.

"Still think we can't keep up with you, Jason?" asked Lindsay as they arrived at the campsite. She was breathing hard from the vigorous hike, but so was everyone else, including the boys.

Before Jason could reply, Mrs. Phillips spoke up. "That's not what this weekend is all about. You are all going to have to work together in order to pass some of the survival skills we'll be working on. It's not going to be boys against girls. In fact, I've selected the teams, and there are two boys and two girls on each team."

"Tell us the teams, Mrs. Phillips," said Todd.

"Todd, Rob, Lindsay, and Jennie are on one team. Jason, Matt, Melanie, and Tara are on the other. You're not really competing against one another, but both teams will be put through the same wilderness survival tests. It's going to take real teamwork to get through them."

"Melanie and I were planning on sharing a tent. Can we still do that, even though we're on different teams?" asked Jennie.

"Sure. You only need to stick with your teams during planned activities."

"Let's set up our tents," suggested Matt.

The students took off in pairs to claim tent sites. The campground was large enough to hold three times as many tents, but all of the students pitched their tents in one area. Mrs. Phillips pitched her tent at the other end of the campground, wanting some privacy.

Later that day Mrs. Phillips sent the teams on a compass-reading activity that took Rob's group to a large rock formation right near the cabin.

"I wish we could just look inside the cabin," said Lindsay.

"Me, too. I've been thinking about it all day. Maybe old Mr. Carver hid some money under a mattress and forgot about it. You hear about people doing that all the time," said Rob.

"It could be in a book," offered Jennie. "He was a writer. I bet he put it in a book."

"Somebody would have found it long ago," said Todd.

"Not necessarily. The cabin's been locked up," said Lindsay.

"Let's go take a look. Maybe there's a loose board or something," said Rob.

"We don't have time. We were due back ten minutes ago," said Jennie, looking at her watch.

Reluctantly, the foursome hiked back to camp.

❖ ❖ ❖

That night the group sat around a cozy campfire telling scary stories and sick jokes. Rob hardly heard a single story because he just couldn't get that cabin out of his mind.

"Jason, come here. I need to talk to you," whispered Rob.

The two boys got up and left.

"I want to see what's inside that old cabin," said Rob.

"But Mrs. Phillips said . . . "

"I know. Forget Mrs. Phillips for a minute. We could go there tonight, after everyone's asleep, and check it out. I think we could pry loose one of the boards with a hammer."

"It's really dark out," said Jason.

"So, we'll take our flashlights. You can see the cabin from the trail."

"Lindsay and Tara might want to come with us. They seemed very curious about the cabin," said Jason.

"Yeah, and Lindsay's light. We could boost her up to one of the windows, and she could pry loose a board and look inside," added Rob.

Lindsay and Tara were intrigued with the idea of sneaking out of camp and exploring the cabin. When the fire was out and everyone had turned in for the night, Jason and Rob tiptoed over to the girls' tent. Flashlights and hammer in hand, all four of them quietly stumbled their way out of camp.

They reached the cabin without incident and began poking and prying the boards covering the windows.

"I feel like a criminal," said Tara.

"Me, too," agreed Lindsay.

"We'll be in so much trouble if Mrs. Phillips catches us," whispered Tara.

"Why are you two whispering? Camp is a half of a mile away," said Jason.

"Hey, guys, this board is loose," said Rob, shining his light on the back window.

They were completely engrossed in accomplishing their task when they heard the unmistakable noise of two dirt bikes coming up the road. Soon they were nearly blinded by two bright lights.

"Quick, hide behind these bushes!" whispered Lindsay.

Four teenagers had never moved so fast. They turned off their flashlights and hugged the damp ground, their hearts pounding. As they lay there, two rather tall figures parked the bikes and took off their helmets. The headlights from their dirt bikes provided all the light they needed to open the padlock.

"The skinny one's a girl," whispered Tara.

"No way. It's two guys," argued Jason.

Both riders were dressed in jeans with leather jackets and boots.

"What do you think they're doing in there?" asked Rob.

"Why are they here in the middle of the night?" wondered Lindsay out loud.

Minutes later the two emerged from the cabin in wet suits and wearing diving gear. It was now obvious that one of them was a woman, the other a man. The guy turned off the bike lights. Both moved quickly and quietly, carrying some kind of equipment in a small, rubber raft.

"What are they planning to do?" asked Lindsay.

"That one piece of equipment looks like a pump or vacuum," said Rob.

"How can you tell?" asked Tara.

"I'm only guessing, but look at those hoses. They're just like the ones that go to our pool vacuum," answered Rob.

Thinking they were completely alone in the woods, the man and woman did not bother to lock the cabin door when they left.

"Let's split up. Two of us can follow them to see what they're doing, and two of us will check out the cabin," said Rob.

"I want to follow them," said Tara.

"I'll go with her," offered Jason.

"Be careful, you guys, and make sure they don't see you," warned Rob.

Rob and Lindsay cautiously stepped into the screened porch and shined their flashlights all around.

"What's this sparkly stuff on the table?" asked Lindsay.

Tiny, gold flecks of something sparkled under the beam of their flashlights.

"I don't know. Let's go inside and look around."

Once inside, they could see that the cabin had been stripped of all furniture. The walls were completely bare. Only a sink with a pump remained in the section of the cabin which must have served as a kitchen. As they continued to shine their lights around the one-room cabin, they found a large, wooden storage cabinet. It was locked with a padlock very much like the one on the cabin door.

"I wonder what's in there?" whispered Lindsay.

"Judging by the size of that lock, it must be something valuable," said Rob.

The two continued their inspection of the cabin. Over in the corner they found two piles of clothing.

"Maybe there's a wallet in these jeans. We could find out who they are," said Rob.

"Do you really think we should?" asked Lindsay.

"You heard Mrs. Phillips. This place is supposed to be boarded up. I don't know what these two are doing here, but I think we should find out who they are and tell Mrs. Phillips."

"You mean admit that we came here tonight?"

"We can talk about that later. Shine your light over here, so I can see what I'm doing."

"Check the back pocket."

"Found it," said Rob, pulling out a man's black leather wallet that was badly worn.

"Is there a driver's license?" asked Lindsay, shining the light right on the wallet.

"His name is David Carver."

The words were barely out of his mouth when two large hands grabbed him from behind and pinned him to the floor of the cabin. The woman wrestled Lindsay to the floor and restrained her.

"What do you kids think you're doing?" asked the man in a gruff and angry voice.

"We were just doing some exploring," answered Rob with a shaky voice.

"Where are your parents?"

"They dropped us off for an overnight," lied Lindsay. "My brother and I love to camp, but our parents hate sleeping in tents."

"They're lying," said the woman, tightening her hold on Lindsay.

"Do you think our parents would let us go out this late at night if they were with us?" asked Rob.

"Let's tie them up for now so we can finish our work. We'll decide what to do with them later. They know who I am. That's a problem," said the man, snatching his wallet out of Rob's hand.

Then they grabbed the rest of their gear and left. This time they were careful to lock the door behind them.

Rob and Lindsay lay on the cold, damp floor of the cabin, unable to move or scream or even see one another in the pitch black cabin.

"We've got to get help," said Jason.

"We'll have to find our way back to camp without using our flashlights. We can't risk their seeing us," said Tara.

Thankfully, their eyes had already adjusted to the dark, so they were able to find the trail without too much difficulty. They held on to one another and moved as quickly as they could, afraid to think of what might happen to Rob and Lindsay if they didn't get them some help in time.

A mile walk never seemed so long to Tara and Jason. Finally, they reached the camp.

"Mrs. Phillips, Mrs. Phillips!" called Jason and Tara in a loud whisper. "Wake up! Rob and Lindsay are in trouble!"

"What's happened?" asked Mrs. Phillips, putting on her shoes and scrambling for her flashlight.

Tara and Jason explained the situation to her.

"Wake the others. We have to move quickly," said Mrs. Phillips, trying to stay calm. She huddled her six students together and shared what had happened with them.

"I'd like two of you to go to my car and phone for help."

"We'll go, Mrs. Phillips," volunteered Jennie and Melanie.

"You must be careful girls. Use no flashlights until you reach my car. Open the door and lock yourselves inside while you call 911. Tell them we need the police and possibly medical help, too. We're at the Cambridge School District Outdoor Education Site at Deep Creek. Can you remember all that?"

"Yes," they answered in unison.

"Be careful," she said again, giving them a hug as she sent them on their way.

"Mrs. Phillips, my brother has a dirt bike. I know how to pull the wires from the ignition so they won't be able to go anywhere," said Jason.

"I'm not sure we want to keep them here. It may be safer for all of us if they leave," said Mrs. Phillips, thinking out loud.

"But what if they've hurt Lindsay and Rob?" asked Tara, trembling with fear.

"You mustn't even think that," said Mrs. Phillips.

"We've got to get back to the cabin before that man and woman return," said Jason.

"We'll set a trap for them," said Matt.

Matt, Jason, Tara, and Todd were amazingly calm as they followed Mrs. Phillips down the trail in absolute silence. They did not pass Melanie and Jennie along the way.

"The girls must have made it to the car by now," whispered Todd.

"Either that or they're lost," answered Jason, hoping he was wrong.

All was quiet when they reached the cabin. The door was locked. Jason and Matt quickly positioned themselves on the roof above the door. Matt and Tara took their places on either side of the path that led to the entrance of the cabin. Mrs. Phillips hid herself under the table on the porch. In her hands she held a large, heavy piece of wood. Hearts pounding, hands sweaty, they waited in the dark of the night.

Jason and Todd heard the inevitable sounds of footsteps as the man and woman trudged up the trail carrying their equipment. As they set down their heavy load and moved towards the front door, they tripped and found themselves tangled in fish line. Next, they were blinded by the beams of light coming from Jason's and Todd's flashlights. They dropped their net right over the two confused and disoriented villains. Jason and Todd jumped off the roof and joined Tara and Matt in holding down the corners of the heavy net. Mrs. Phillips stood poised and ready to smack the man and the woman with her club should it be necessary.

The man and the woman squirmed and groaned beneath the net, but it was soon obvious that they weren't going anywhere.

"Rob! Lindsay! Are you all right?" yelled Mrs. Phillips.

There was no reply.

"What have you done to those kids?" demanded Mrs. Phillips.

The man spoke first. "They're O.K. We didn't hurt them. We only tied and gagged them."

"Thank God," said Mrs. Phillips, with tears of joy flooding her eyes.

"Hey, I wonder what happened to Melanie and Jen . . . "

The words were barely out of Todd's mouth when the two girls burst into sight.

"Help's on the way! We got through!" said Melanie, slightly out of breath.

"I'm very proud of all of you," said Mrs. Phillips. "We'll stay right where we are until they get here. We can't take any chances of these two getting away."

Then she called to Rob and Lindsay inside the cabin. "Try to make some kind of sound so we'll know you're O.K."

Everyone got quiet and listened. They were almost sure they heard a banging sound.

"That's probably Rob's hard head," said Jason, and they all laughed and cried at the same time with relief.

The sheriff and one deputy from Dawson, a small town about nine miles from Deep Creek, pulled into the small parking area near the cabin. An ambulance followed closely behind. The sheriff and his deputy couldn't help but grin when they saw the way the six students and their teacher had captured the two culprits.

Sheriff Edward Parnell and his deputy Linda Reynolds took charge. In a matter of seconds they determined that the man and woman were not armed. David Carver and his wife Kay cooperated fully with the police. They turned over the key to the cabin so that Rob and Lindsay could be set free. David Carver turned out to be John Carver's grandson. He had spent many happy days as a child with his grandfather in the cabin. He had always dreamed of mining for gold in Deep Creek. He was bitterly disappointed when his grandfather did not will the cabin to him. His hunch had been right; there was indeed gold at Deep Creek, and he and his wife were using the latest, most sophisticated mining methods to extract the gold.

Lindsay and Rob assured Sheriff Parnell and his deputy that they had not been harmed in any way by the Carvers. They were shaken up and scared, but otherwise no real harm had been done.

"What will happen to them?" asked Rob.

"Well, for starters, they will be charged with trespassing and false imprisonment," answered Deputy Reynolds.

"We'll need to take all of the children down to the station to get their statements, Mrs. Phillips."

"Can it wait till morning? We aren't even dressed."

"It would be best if they could come with us now. By morning they may have forgotten some important details," answered Sheriff Parnell. "If you'd like, you may go back to your tents and change."

"Thank you. Our campsite is about a mile from here."

"Deputy Reynolds and I will secure the cabin and wait with the prisoners."

The students discussed the evening's events in great detail on the trail back to their campsite. Only Mrs. Phillips walked along in silence. Her students were too busy talking to notice that she was very upset about something.

Jason, Rob, Tara, and Lindsay were pretty proud of themselves for having discovered the gold mining operation. It was most likely their boasting that brought Mrs. Phillips's anger and frustration right to the surface where it exploded.

"I hope you've all enjoyed your exciting adventure!"

"What do you mean?" asked Rob.

"I mean, when this hits the newspapers the school board will relinquish their blessing and funds for this Outdoor Education Program. You kids could have been killed. You left camp without permission. Total supervision on an outing like this is virtually impossible. The sponsors have to be able to trust the students and that just doesn't seem possible. Two years ago we started an Outdoor Education Program, and the second group of students we brought to the woods had to be taken home the first night because they brought alcohol with them. The school board very reluctantly gave us a second chance. I'm afraid you've ruined things for everyone now. So, you'll have to forgive me if I don't think this has all been a terribly exciting adventure!"

With that, she unzipped her tent, crawled in it, and began to dress for the sheriff's station.

"Looks like we really blew it this time," said Rob, feeling as awful as he could ever remember feeling about anything.

"I've never seen Mrs. Phillips so upset," said Tara. "She must hate us."

"They shouldn't cancel the whole program just because we made a mistake," said Lindsay. "That's not fair."

"You guys, Mrs. Phillips brought us to this first outing because she trusted us. We really let her down," said Jason.

"I never thought anything like this would happen," said Rob. "All I wanted to do was take a look inside the cabin."

"Let's go get dressed, guys. The sheriff is waiting for us," said Melanie.

Rob, Jason, Tara, and Lindsay apologized to Mrs. Phillips. Realizing how sorry they really were, she forgave her students, and together they anxiously waited to hear from the school board concerning the fate of the Outdoor Education Program.

Topics One, Two, and Three:

SCHOOL BOARD MEMBER INTERVIEW
Time: Three 25-minute sessions

MATERIALS NEEDED:
- videotape of a school board meeting
- interview questions
- school board member

DIRECTIONS:

Students will prepare to hold a mock school board meeting to decide the fate of the Outdoor Education Program at Jerome Middle School.

1. Obtain a videotape of one of your local school board meetings. Select a short segment to familiarize students with the activities of a school board member.

2. Invite a local school board member to speak to your class.

3. Conduct a large group discussion to determine questions students will include in their interview with the school board member.

POSSIBLE QUESTIONS:
- What are the qualifications needed to be a school board member?
- Were you elected or appointed to office?
- How long does each board member serve?
- What are your duties as a school board member?
- How does a school board make decisions?

Topic Four: MOCK SCHOOL BOARD MEETING

Time: Two 25-minute sessions

MATERIALS NEEDED:

- ticket sheet (pages 124 and 125)

DIRECTIONS:

Students will conduct a mock school board meeting to decide the fate of the Outdoor Education Program for Jerome Middle School.

1. Assign student roles for the mock meeting by choice or by random selection using the names provided on the ticket sheet.

2. Students speak before the board, presenting their viewpoints according to their chosen or assigned roles. The teacher may want to set a time limit for each speaker.

3. All students in the class participate in the mock meeting. (See ticket sheet, pages 124 and 125.)

4. Allow students 5–10 minutes to prepare arguments for or against continuing the Outdoor Education Program.

5. School board members should use this time to elect a president who will conduct the meeting.

6. The undecided participants list the pros and cons of continuing the program. They will form their opinions by listening to all of the arguments presented, and then present to the group.

7. After listening to each class member speak, the school board votes and announces the outcome to the class.

TICKET SHEET FOR "DEEP CREEK"

School Board Member

School Board Member

School Board Member

School Board Member

School Board Member

Superintendent of Schools

Jerome Middle School Principal

Mrs. Phillips—The Outdoor Education Teacher

Former Teacher with
Outdoor Education Experience
*(She was the teacher when students brought
alcohol to the last outdoor education experience.)*

Rob—Talked Jason, Lindsay, and Tara
into exploring the cabin

Jason—One of four students who
explored the cabin

Lindsay—One of four students who
explored the cabin

Tara—One of four students who
explored the cabin

Matt—Went on trip and obeyed the
rules

Todd—Went on trip and obeyed the
rules

Jennie—Went on trip and obeyed the
rules

TICKET SHEET FOR "DEEP CREEK"

Melanie—Went on trip and obeyed the rules

Outraged Parent—Thinks the Outdoor Education Program is too dangerous

Supportive Parent—Thinks the Outdoor Education Program is a worthwhile experience

Outraged Parent—Thinks the Outdoor Education Program is too dangerous

Supportive Parent—Thinks the Outdoor Education Program is a worthwhile experience

Undecided—Listens to arguments before the board and makes a decision before speaking

Undecided—Listens to arguments before the board and makes a decision before speaking

Undecided—Listens to arguments before the board and makes a decision before speaking

Undecided—Listens to arguments before the board and makes a decision before speaking

Undecided—Listens to arguments before the board and makes a decision before speaking

Undecided—Listens to arguments before the board and makes a decision before speaking

ABSENCE
OF
INTEGRITY

"Mrs. Phillips?"

"Yes."

"Will you please send Jason to the office? Mrs. Baker needs to see him," came the booming voice of Mrs. Brown, the school secretary, over the loud speaker."

"Ooh, somebody's in big trouble!" snickered half the class.

"Quiet down," warned Mrs. Phillips. "Yes, Mrs. Brown, he's on his way."

Jason grabbed his books and his backpack and left the room. He had a pretty good idea why he had been called to the office, but he hoped he was wrong.

"Maybe she just wants to congratulate me for not getting sent to her office in over a month," he tried to convince himself."

It was a short walk to the office, too short as far as Jason was concerned. As he approached the outer door, he took a deep breath and tried his hardest to look as though he were incapable of whatever it was he might be accused of doing.

"Have a seat in the third office, Jason. Mrs. Baker will be right with you," said Mrs. Brown.

"Yes, ma'am," answered Jason as he walked into the small, stuffy room that contained only one small table and two chairs. He dropped his backpack on the floor, pulled out the chair closest to him, and sat down. He sat there for what seemed like an hour, and still no sight of Mrs. Baker. His eyelids began to get heavy, and he felt so sleepy he couldn't keep his eyes open.

"I'll just rest my head on the table," he thought. Then, he drifted off to dreamland . . .

❖ ❖ ❖

It was an ordinary day at Jerome Middle School. As the bell rang, the students lined up in alphabetical order outside their first period classrooms. When the teacher, Mrs. Phillips, opened the door, she scrutinized the students as they filed through the doorway.

The students carried their books in a stack. No backpacks, purses, or athletic bags were allowed on campus, for obvious reasons. Everyone knew students were not to be trusted. Years ago, when they were permitted to carry all types of bags, students concealed food, drugs, alcohol, gum, stolen paper and pencils, radios, and even stolen books. How foolish people were back then to think that anyone could be trusted to carry only what belonged to them. How stupid they must have been to allow students to carry these devices of deception.

Most of the students were allowed to take their seats. Three students were asked to empty their pockets because they seemed to be carrying more in their pockets than the required supplies.

"All right, empty your pockets," ordered Mrs. Phillips.

Sarah, a rather pretty girl with long blond hair, began. She pulled out her pencil, a pen, an eraser, her lunch tickets, and a bottle of contact lens solution.

"What's in that bottle?"

"It's solution for my contacts," replied Sarah.

"Let me see your permit for carrying it."

Sarah opened her notebook. The permit was clipped to her student I.D. card.

"You may sit down, Sarah. Carl, you're next. Please hurry."

Obediently, Carl quickly took out a pencil, a pen, an eraser, and his lunch ticket.

"Keep going. It looks like you have something more."

Reluctantly, Carl reached down deep into his pocket. He produced a hollow cylinder that was once a pen. He also pulled out three small balls of clay. Without saying a word, Mrs. Phillips called security to have Carl removed from the classroom. He would serve three days of in-school suspension for his offense.

Every eye in the class was now turned toward Allan, a new student. He looked embarrassed. Like the others, he pulled out all the required supplies from his pockets, but then he produced a stack of baseball cards held together with a rubber band.

"Bring those cards to me. Carrying a rubber band is against Jerome's rules. Didn't the counselor explain our rules to you?"

"Yes, ma'am, he did, but I guess I forgot. I only meant to use the rubber band to keep my collection of baseball cards together. I'm sorry."

Years ago, when teachers believed students, Allan might have gotten away with breaking this rule, but teachers had gotten wise over the years. Even the most sincere-looking student didn't have a chance to explain or give excuses.

"How unfortunate for you, Allan. I was hoping you would turn out to be a more cooperative student," replied Mrs. Phillips. "Since you are new here, I will not send you to in-school suspension this time, but I will have to confiscate your baseball cards. Your parents may pick them up at the office, minus the rubber band, of course." With that, she grabbed her scissors and cut the rubber band in two.

"Thank you, Mrs. Phillips," said Allan, relieved at not being sent to in-school suspension. Allan had been diagnosed as hyperactive by several doctors, so being confined to a small room for an entire day was more than he could endure.

Mrs. Phillips walked over to her desk to get her language arts textbook. She had her back turned only for an instant, but still, it was enough time for Bob Thomas to get out his pen and write an obscene word on the desk next to his. As he reached over, he left his back pocket exposed. The student sitting behind him, a sly girl named Lisa, snatched his lunch ticket. Kelly and John saw both of these pranks occurring, but said nothing.

"Class, please get out your paper and head it correctly. You will be taking notes all hour." The students mumbled their complaints, but everyone complied.

Mrs. Phillips went on and on spewing out one boring piece of information after another in her usual manner. The students were writing as fast as they could. Their hands were aching and the points of their pencils were getting dull. Just when things couldn't get worse, Mrs. Phillips started using fifty cent words, which most of the kids couldn't even begin to spell correctly.

"Mrs. Phillips, could you please write some of the terms on the board for us?" asked a frustrated student. "I can't even read what I'm writing."

"Of course I can," began Mrs. Phillips, feeling sorry for her students. But then she remembered what had happened the last time she turned her back on the class to write on the chalkboard. Two students had stolen her stapler. "You'll just have to spell them the best you can," said Mrs. Phillips. "I'd be asking for trouble to turn my back on the class."

Moments later, the bell rang. Mrs. Phillips looked over the desks before dismissing the class. "Everyone may go, except for Mike Larson," announced Mrs. Phillips with authority.

Mike sat there with a puzzled look on his face. "Why are you keeping me?"

"Don't try to play dumb with me. Did you think I wouldn't notice the filthy little graffiti on the side of your desk?"

Mike could feel anger welling up inside of him. How could he be so stupid? How could he have let somebody get away with writing on his desk? He knew how important it was to watch every move his fellow students made. Knowing it was useless to deny the charge, Mike took his punishment. He would have to wash the desks in Mrs. Phillips's room every night for a week. Sometimes it was really awful to live in a society where a person's word meant nothing.

Mike left the classroom, leaving Mrs. Phillips alone. She picked up her keys and locked her file cabinet, the book closet, and all of her desk drawers. Then, she gathered up her papers and her purse and headed for the teachers' lunchroom. Gone was the spring in her step and the laughter in her voice. She walked cautiously and with purpose, hoping to reach the lunchroom without having to call security. Lately, there had been an outbreak of attacks; students who just couldn't cope any longer with the rigors of school had been attacking other students and stealing their homework.

The halls appeared to be quiet. As Mrs. Phillips neared the lunchroom, she noticed Jennie, one of her students, sitting alone under a tree. It looked as though she had been crying. Mrs. Phillips had always suspected that Jennie was an especially sensitive child. She decided to go over to Jennie to find out what seemed to be troubling her.

"Jennie, is everything all right?" asked Mrs. Phillips with kindness in her voice, a kindness she was not permitted to display in the classroom.

"I'm O.K.," lied Jennie.

"Do you mind if I sit with you? It's not really a good idea for you to be out here alone."

"No, I don't mind."

Mrs. Phillips took out her sandwich and began eating. "Have you eaten? Would you like half? My husband always makes a great sandwich."

"I'm not really hungry. I never can eat when I'm upse . . . "

"So, something is wrong. What is it? You seemed fine during class this morning."

"I got in trouble in science today for something I didn't do. Everyone saw what really happened, but no one would tell, not that the teacher would listen. Mr. Fenwick thinks I turned the gas on at my station, but I didn't do it. I saw Brad Watson fooling around at my station. He did it, but I'm getting suspended for it. Mr. Fenwick never even asked me or any of the other students what happened."

"It's school policy not to ask. You know that, Jennie."

"Well, I think it's a dumb policy. I'm going to be in a lot of trouble when my dad gets here. He'll have to leave work to pick me up. He has a new job, and he's trying to make a good impression. I can already see the worried look he'll have in his eyes," said Jennie with a troubled voice.

"Jennie, it didn't used to be this way. We used to talk to students whenever we had problems in class, but it just didn't work out. The students who got into trouble lied about what really happened."

"Yes, but what about the students around them? Didn't they speak up and tell the teacher the truth?"

"Absolutely not. There was a strong code among the students which forbade telling on another student if it meant that student would get in trouble. So, we just quit asking."

"When will your father be here?"

"I'm not sure. They weren't able to reach him. He was in a meeting."

"Maybe it's not too late then, Jennie. I might be able to go to the office and speak on your behalf. Mr. Fenwick and I have been teaching together a long time. If I can get him to withdraw his accusation, you'll be off the hook."

"Thank you, Mrs. Phillips. I really appreciate it."

"Don't thank me yet. It's highly unlikely that I'll succeed, but I'll give it my best. If the office doesn't notify you about your father, you'll know Mr. Fenwick agreed."

Mrs. Phillips walked down to Mr. Fenwick's room and found him grading papers. He admitted that he hadn't actually seen Jennie turn on the gas. He reluctantly walked to the office and tore up his report on the incident.

Mrs. Phillips had very little time to finish her lunch, but somehow that didn't matter to her. She got her energy to teach that afternoon from the warmth she felt inside from helping Jennie. She could be mistaken, but in subsequent days, she thought she felt a special bond between Jennie and herself. She had to be careful not to let her guard down. Other teachers had been tricked before by students they had begun to trust. She knew it was dangerous to believe that Jennie was different, yet still, it had been years since she had felt that way about one of her students, and she seemed to be more alive because of it.

The following week, Mrs. Phillips decided to show a film in class. They had just finished reading *A Separate Peace* and she thought her students would enjoy seeing the movie which was made from the book. Teachers could apply for clearance to turn off the lights and show a film if they felt they had a class that would focus on the movie and not on the opportunity to vandalize and steal in the darkness. Of course, extra security would be necessary. Two security guards would be assigned to help assure the well-being of all students.

Mrs. Phillips taught six classes throughout the day. Two of those classes would be allowed to see the film. She just felt it would be too risky to turn the lights off in her other classes. Jennie's class was one of the two classes she thought she could trust.

As the students enthusiastically filed into class, they were frisked by security—the girls by a female guard named Mrs. Elroy, and the boys by a male guard named Mr. Jordan. Since films were a rare occurrence, the students really looked forward to them. Everyone cooperated with the guards, and Mrs. Phillips was able to start the film.

Several minutes into the film, Mrs. Phillips looked around the classroom. Everyone was engrossed in the story. It gave her a chance to relax and catch up on some grading. She sat in the back of the room. A small, battery-operated reading lamp provided just enough light for her to check the students' papers and record the scores in her grade book. She was working quickly, hoping to finish at least two class sections, when she heard the scream.

"Get the lights!" she shouted. Mr. Jordan quickly flipped the light switch. Tara, a girl who was sitting in the fifth seat of the third row, was holding her hand over her eye. She was crying out in pain.

"Someone shot me with a rubber band! I'm hurt! I can't see!"

Mrs. Phillips went over to try to comfort the poor girl. Mrs. Elroy pushed the emergency button to let the school nurse know she was needed immediately. The students sat quietly in their desks, realizing the gravity of the situation.

Miss Sheldon, the school nurse, soon appeared. She took one look at Tara's eye and decided to call for an ambulance. "I'm afraid she's going to need surgery. I'd rather not move her. I think we'd better wait for the ambulance right here."

Minutes later, the paramedics arrived and rushed Tara to the emergency room. It was then that Mrs. Phillips addressed the class.

"Who did this?"

Silence.

"Who did this? Who shot a rubber band?" asked Mrs. Phillips in a rather shrill voice that indicated just how upset she was over this.

More silence.

"Mrs. Phillips, we'll have to search each student," said Mrs. Elroy. "Perhaps we'll locate another rubber band."

The students emptied their pockets and at first nothing was found. Then, Jason stepped up to empty his pockets. He walked over to Mr. Jordan and just stood there. As he reached into his pocket, his face grew pale. He slowly brought his hand out of his pocket, and there they were—three red rubber bands.

"Come with us," ordered the security guards.

"I didn't shoot Tara. I admit, I was planning to have a little fun during the movie, but I got so interested in the movie that I forgot all about the rubber bands. Please, you've got to believe me," he pleaded.

"Let's go, Jason. You are obviously guilty. Don't make things worse for yourself," advised Mrs. Elroy. Then, the two guards led Jason out of the classroom and down the hall to the principal's office.

Trying to regain her composure, Mrs. Phillips addressed the class. "I know you are very upset and worried about Tara. As soon as we have any information about her, we'll share it with you."

"Do you think Tara will be blind in that eye?" asked one of the students.

"I hope not," answered Mrs. Phillips. Before she could say anything else, the bell rang, and she dismissed the class. As her students left the classroom, Mrs. Phillips noticed that Jennie seemed to be particularly upset.

"She's such a sweet, sensitive girl," thought Mrs. Phillips to herself.

The next day the school received word from Tara's parents that she most likely would not lose her vision in her injured eye. The doctors weren't positive, but the prognosis was encouraging. She would have to spend the next several days in the hospital to recover from the eye surgery. Mrs. Phillips passed along the good news to her students. She also had some bad news for them.

"Jason will not be returning to our class. Because of the seriousness of his actions, he will be attending Anderson Alternative School where the security is much greater. At this time I must also inform you that I will no longer be your language arts instructor. I will finish out this week, and then another teacher will take my place. The administration feels that I used poor judgment in allowing this class to watch a film. Jason had been involved in a few minor incidents before. They feel that I should have sent someone with Jason's background to a study hall. Since he seriously hurt another student as the result of my negligence, I will no longer be teaching. I thought you had the right to understand the procedure because you are directly affected."

Most of the students just sat there, not really sure what to say.

"Mrs. Phillips, if it had been another student who hurt Tara, one who had never been in trouble before, would you still lose your job?" asked Jennie.

"No, I would not. I would just have received a written reprimand advising me to be more careful in the future," she answered.

Mrs. Phillips went through the motions of teaching her classes that day, but she was definitely not herself. She had been teaching for fifteen years, and suddenly she found herself out of work with no real idea of what kind of career she could pursue. She had always wanted to be a teacher—ever since she could remember.

At the end of the day, just as she was getting ready to leave, she heard a knock at her door.

"Come in," she yelled. There in the doorway stood Jennie.

"Hello, Mrs. Phillips. I just wanted to tell you how sorry I am about what happened. I think you're a really good teacher, and I'm going to miss you."

"Thank you, Jennie. It's very kind of you to stop by."

"What will you do?"

"I'm not sure, Jennie, but don't worry about me. I'll be fine."

"Well, good-bye. I'll see you tomorrow," said Jennie.

"Bye, Jennie."

Jennie walked down the hall to her locker. Her friend Ellen was waiting for her. She was talking with two other students about what had happened to Jason and Mrs. Phillips. She joined them just as Ellen was saying how lucky she was not to have gotten caught shooting her rubber band at Tara.

"You mean it was you and not Jason?" asked Jennie in disbelief.

"Yeah, it was me, but I never meant to hurt her. I feel just awful about her eye, but I'm going to bring her some flowers in the hospital tonight."

"We've got to go or we'll miss our bus," yelled the other two girls. They ran off, leaving Jennie and Ellen alone.

"We better hurry, too. The guards will be along any minute to lock the area," said Ellen.

Jennie and Ellen had been good friends for a little over a year. Ellen had always been popular at school, but Jennie was always rather shy. She didn't really gain acceptance from the other kids at school until Ellen had started paying attention to her. Ellen lived just three houses down from her, and they had become good friends because it was so easy for them to get together, and because they really liked each other. No matter how worried and down Jennie felt, Ellen could always cheer her up.

As the two girls walked home together that night, they continued to talk about what had happened in Mrs. Phillips's class.

"Why didn't you tell me that you shot Tara?"

"I don't know. I guess I was just feeling too awful about it. I never meant to hurt her. It was just supposed to be a joke. When she screamed, I got so scared. Luckily, I had only brought one rubber band with me, so when they searched us, I was clean."

"Don't you feel bad about Jason? He's in so much trouble, and he didn't do anything," said Jennie.

"Well, at first I felt bad, but then I got to thinking. He did have rubber bands, and he did plan on shooting them. It could just as well have been him. Besides, you know the rules. We students aren't trusted. Even if I had said I did it, they wouldn't believe me. They have no evidence that I did it. No one would suspect me. After all, Tara and I are good friends."

"What about Mrs. Phillips? She's getting fired over this mess. You heard in class today. If it had been a student with no previous record, she would only have gotten a reprimand."

"I was feeling guilty about her losing her job, but then I heard a bunch of kids from our class talking, and most of them are glad she's leaving. She gives too much homework, and her tests are very hard."

"Well, I like her. She's got a pretty good sense of humor, and she's really nice outside of the classroom."

"What do you mean?" asked Ellen.

"Remember that day Mr. Fenwick was going to have me suspended for turning on the gas jets, and she got him to drop the accusation?"

"Oh, yeah, I forgot about that," said Ellen. "I guess she is pretty nice. How was I supposed to know they were going to fire her?"

"There must be something we can do to straighten this whole thing out," said Jennie.

"Like what, Jen?"

"Like tell what really happened."

"What? Are you crazy? No one in my family ever gets in trouble. I can't do that."

"Mrs. Phillips might understand and . . ."

"No one is going to listen to Mrs. Phillips. They'll think she put us up to it to save her job."

"You're probably right," agreed Jennie.

"Promise me you won't tell, Jen. You're one of my best friends. I thought I could trust you."

"You can. Don't worry, I won't say anything."

The two girls walked along in silence. After a few minutes, Ellen broke the silence. "Look, Jen, I know you're a little upset about this. The first time I kept quiet when I knew the truth, I felt just like you. Trust me. It gets a little easier each time," she said with confidence.

"The next time . . ." thought Jennie. "There isn't going to be a next time." But as she continued walking with Ellen, she knew it would happen AGAIN, and AGAIN, and AGAIN, and AGAIN . . .

"Wake up, Jason," said Mrs. Brown, shaking Jason's arm.

Jason jumped up out of his chair with a start. "What's going on? Where am I?"

"You're in the office. You must have fallen asleep. I think you were having a bad dream. It is rather stuffy in this little room. Mrs. Baker is ready to see you now. Go right into her office."

"Yes, ma'am."

"Jason, I have been informed by a couple of students that you have been throwing dirt clods at the buses after school," said Mrs. Baker. "My sources are very reliable, but I thought I should ask you first before giving you your punishment. Are they telling the truth?"

"Thanks for asking me, Mrs. Baker. I'm afraid it's true."

Jason's admission of guilt took Mrs. Baker completely by surprise.

"Thank you for your honesty, Jason. I must say it's very refreshing."

"What are you going to do to me?"

"I'm giving you three days of lunch clean-up. I usually assign a week, but because of your honesty, I'm giving you a break."

"Thanks, Mrs. Baker," said Jason. Then, he picked up his backpack and headed back to class.

┌─Topic One: **RIPPLE EFFECT OF "A LACK OF INTEGRITY"**─┐
Time: 20–25 minutes

MATERIALS NEEDED:
- Ripple Effect activity sheet (page 139, one per group)

Small Group Activity

DIRECTIONS:

1. Students form groups of no more than four.
2. Each group needs a Ripple Effect sheet.
3. Students discuss how each of the characters in the story was affected by the lack of integrity that occurred in the classroom.
4. The group decides who was most affected and places that name in the center of the ripples.
5. The students continue to place characters in the ripples, with the character being least affected placed in the outside ripple.
6. When each group has completed the Ripple Effect activity sheet, one person from each group reports the results to the class for comparison and discussion by the large group.

Place the following characters on the Ripple Effect activity sheet:

Jason:	falsely accused of shooting the rubber band
Mrs. Phillips:	teacher who lost her job
Jennie:	discovers the truth but doesn't tell
Ellen:	shot the rubber band and kept quiet about it
Tara:	nearly lost her eye

RIPPLE EFFECT ACTIVITY SHEET

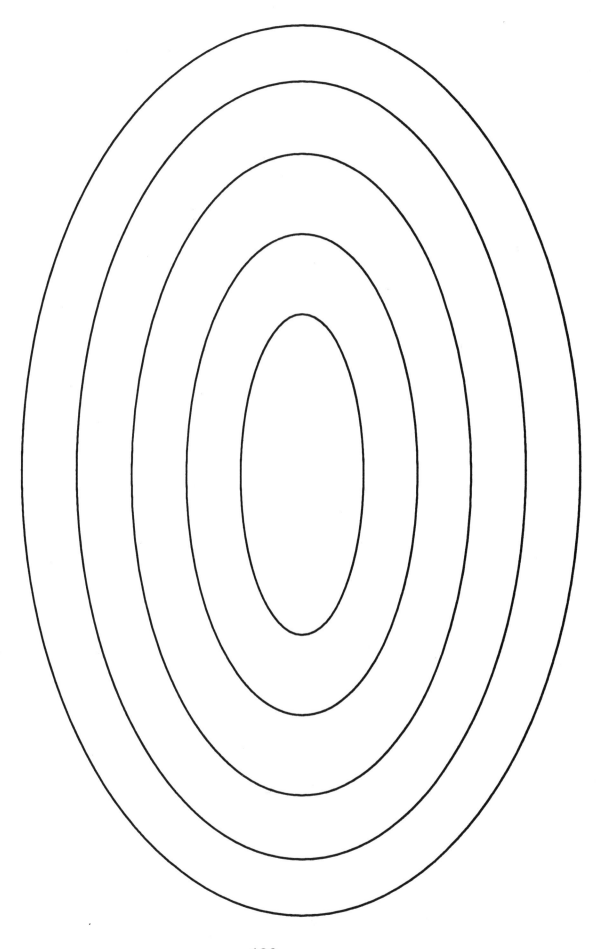

——— Topic Two: **CONCENTRATION GAME** ———
Time: 20–25 minutes

MATERIALS NEEDED:

- Concentration Game activity sheets (pages 141 and 142, one set intact to study per group and one set cut up for the game per group)

Small Group Activity

DIRECTIONS:

1. Prepare the cards for the Concentration Game by cutting up one set of words and definitions for each group.

2. Students form groups of no more than four.

3. Give each group a copy of the Concentration Game activity sheet to study the words and their corresponding definitions. Allow five minutes.

4. Pass out Concentration Game Cards.

5. Students shuffle cards and place them face down.

6. The object of the game is to match words with their definitions.

7. The student whose first name is closest to the letter "I" in the alphabet will go first.

8. The first player will turn over two cards. If they match, the player is allowed to keep the cards and continue playing. If they do not match, the player turns them back over, and the play passes to the player on the right.

9. Play continues until all of the cards are matched. The player with the most cards wins.

CONCENTRATION GAME SHEET

ACCUSE	TO CHARGE WITH AN ERROR
ADMIT	TO CONFESS THE TRUTH
COURAGE	ABILITY TO FACE DANGER WITH CONFIDENCE
COWARD	ONE WHO LACKS COURAGE
DECEIVE	TO MAKE SOMEONE BELIEVE SOMETHING THAT IS NOT TRUE
EXAGGERATE	TO MAKE APPEAR GREATER THAN IT IS; OVERSTATE

CONCENTRATION GAME SHEET

FRAME	**TO INCRIMINATE SOMEONE FALSELY**
HONEST	**DISPLAYING TRUTHFULNESS**
IMPLICATE	**TO INVOLVE OR CONNECT WITH A CRIME**
INTEGRITY	**STRICT PERSONAL HONESTY**
SELF-RESPECT	**PROPER RESPECT FOR ONESELF**
SLY	**SNEAKY AND UNDERHANDED**
TRUST	**FAITH OR BELIEF IN SOMEONE**

Topic Three: **INTEGRITY PICTURE**
Time: 25 minutes

MATERIALS NEEDED:
- paper
- markers, colored pencils, or crayons

DIRECTIONS:

1. Each student draws a picture showing how life would be different if everyone had integrity. Students may draw one picture or a series of cartoons. Their work may show comparison/contrast. For example: lockers with and without locks, money earned and money stolen, students doing their own work and students copying, etc.

2. Optional follow-up activities:
   - Have each student write a story to accompany his or her picture, using the picture as a cover for the story.
   - Have the class make a collage for the classroom with their pictures.
   - The class can bind their pictures together into a book.
   - The class can select one or more drawings to print in the school newspaper.
   - Interested students can write an editorial for the school newspaper about integrity at school and can include an illustration.